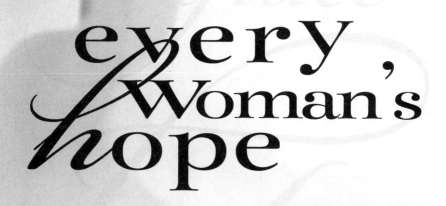

every,
Woman's
hope

defined by grace

every, Woman's hope

beloved by God

HOWARD®
PUBLISHING CO.

Lisa Harper

Our purpose at Howard Publishing is to:

- *Increase faith* in the hearts of growing Christians
- *Inspire holiness* in the lives of believers
- *Instill hope* in the hearts of struggling people everywhere

Because He's coming again!

Every Woman's Hope © 2001 by Lisa Harper
All rights reserved. Printed in the United States of America

Published by Howard Publishing Co., Inc.
3117 North 7th Street, West Monroe, Louisiana 71291-2227

01 02 03 04 05 06 07 08 09 10   10 9 8 7 6 5 4 3 2 1

Edited by Michele Buckingham
Interior design by Stephanie Denney

Library of Congress Cataloging-in-Publication Data
Harper, Lisa, 1963-
   Every woman's hope : defined by grace, beloved by God / Lisa Harper.
      p. cm.
   ISBN 1-58229-190-X
      1. Women—Religious life. I. Title.
   BV4527 .H37 2001
   248.8'43—dc21   2001024572

Scripture taken from the Holy Bible, New International Version. Copyright © 1973, 1978, 1984 International Bible Society. Used by permission of Zondervan Bible Publishers.

To my mom,
Patti Angel,
who taught me about Jesus

Contents

Part 3: *beloved by God*

Special thanks to

Kim Hill, whose friendship
is one of my sweetest earthly treasures

Judy B. Flaherty, who exemplifies steadfast love

Theresa H. Bruno, my sister and cheerleader

E. Andrew Harper, my tender-hearted father

Julie Dilworth, Wendy Martin, Pammy Markle,
and Marcia Strickland

Darlene Grieme, Eva Whittington Self, and
Cindy McDaniel, for much love, prayer, and laughter

Denny and Philis Boultinghouse at Howard Publishing

Wes Yoder and Naomi Duncan at Ambassador Agency

Michele Buckingham, a gracious editor with a light touch

And the wonderful staff and good friends at
Christ Presbyterian Church

Introduction

This may sound strange, but my mind has been greatly affected by a frog named Jeremiah. I'd better explain! When my sister, Theresa, and I were growing up in the late sixties and seventies, Mom didn't allow us to listen to rock music. I guess the television coverage of Woodstock shocked her into thinking that kind of music would do us irreparable harm.

Of course, Theresa and I thought her regulations were far too restrictive, so one day we sweet-talked Dad into buying us an eight-track tape of forbidden fruit. I don't remember any of the songs on the tape except "Joy to the World." You might be familiar with the song; it's considered one of the great rock classics from that era. But the lyrics—about a bullfrog with a biblical name—make no sense whatsoever. However, at eight and twelve, we thought it was an awesome song because there was a line in the chorus that said, "I never understood a single word he said, but I helped him drink his wine, and he always had some mighty fine wine."

To have an "illegal" eight-track was wild enough, but the fact that the song mentioned liquor made us feel like rebels without a cause!

One of my favorite early memories with my sister centers on that silly song. The two of us were sitting in Dad's truck, waiting for him to get out of a meeting, and we were playing that song over and over again as loud as it would go. We had the windows rolled down, and we were singing/screaming every word at the top of our lungs. We even made the "da da dah" noises along with the drumbeat! Dad didn't reprimand us very often, but I remember him striding across the parking lot growling for us to "turn that racket down!"

We played the tape until it dragged and skipped, and we never got tired of singing "Joy to the World." To this day, whenever I hear the word *frog* or meet someone named Jeremiah, I usually grin and start humming that song in my head. Our assistant pastor has a son named Jeremiah, and every time I see him or say hi, I have to remind myself not to launch into a song-and-dance routine!

It's almost as if that song got permanently recorded on a "tape" in my mind. I think we all have a kind of tape in our heads that "lyrics" get recorded on. Some of our songs are fun and harmless, like my ode to amphibians. And some evoke warm, special memories. But some of the messages we've heard damage our hearts, especially the recordings that distort the way we think God views us.

I had lunch with a group of women recently, and our conversation turned to weight. I was the only person at the table who wasn't rail-thin, and I was the only one eating a sandwich instead of a salad! Anyway, a petite woman regaled the rest of us with the horror story of how much weight she'd gained during her last pregnancy. The climax of her story was when she told us the amount she weighed right before the baby was born. When she mouthed the number of pounds, everyone gasped in disbelief. They just couldn't imagine her that huge. I almost choked on my chicken salad when she revealed her tipping-the-scales-with-baby weight because it was the exact same number I'd just given the diet counselor at Jenny Craig for my weight goal!

Those precious women have a script that plays in their subconsciouses saying they're more lovable if they're really lean. Their self-worth isn't based securely on God's love; it's based partly on their dress size. Most of us are no different. It's our deepest desire and greatest hope to be loved well, especially by God. But we aren't sure we're worth His effort. We usually "hear" God on a mental tape that drags and skips. We listen to discordant versions of the beautiful melody He's arranged for us. We don't hear the wonderful words of delight the prophet Zephaniah says He sings over us. We place our value in our appearance or performance instead of in His promise to take pleasure in those who put their hope in Him. And we don't begin to see ourselves with

God's mercy. Most of us have a very hard time believing we're His beloved.

My hope for this book is that it will help you hear His voice more clearly. I pray that somehow God empowers these pages to remind you of how very much He loves you. My purpose in writing one more book among millions is that some woman somewhere will pick it up and hear music she's never heard before or has long forgotten, sung from the lips of the Lord Who adores her. And when she hears His endearments, she will begin to hope again. Because even though we are all desperate for mercy, we are defined by grace and beloved by God. And His love for His daughters is immensely greater than *every woman's hope*.

Part 1: desperate for mercy

Self is the opaque veil that hides the
Face of God from us.

—Richard Foster
Spiritual Classics

ONE

Crippled by Sin

Pantyhose and Pardons

If life really does imitate art, then mine could often be mistaken for a comedy. Instead of being the model of flawless decorum and perfect disposition, I frequently expose my desperate need for help! One of my more humorous displays of desperation happened a few years ago when I was on staff with Focus on the Family in Colorado Springs. I had the opportunity to work at Focus with Dr. James Dobson for six years, so it was a bittersweet experience when it came time for me to leave and start a new job in Nashville, Tennessee. I was excited about moving back to Nashville, but I was sad about leaving my friends in Colorado. Therefore, the last few weeks were a blur of social activity, as I tried to see as many friends as possible before moving across the country.

One afternoon I was walking back toward my office from the ladies' room when I ran into a man who worked in the department next to mine. I was glad to see him because we both traveled a lot on business and I wasn't sure we'd have the chance to say good-bye. We started talking about my departure and how God orders our steps and directs our paths and how we can rest in the knowledge of His sovereignty. I was absorbed in our conversation, thinking how fortunate I had been to work with people like him; however, I was a little distracted by the fact that he wouldn't look directly at me. I kept trying to position myself so that he'd have to meet my eyes, but he kept looking out over the horizon of cubicles just beyond us. He's kind of a biblical scholar, so I thought he might be pondering some deep theological point, and that's why he wouldn't look at me. We said our good-byes after a few minutes, and he turned and walked briskly toward his office.

As I turned to walk to mine, I felt a cool breeze on my legs and looked down to find them uncovered—completely uncovered. I was mortified to realize that I'd accidentally tucked my skirt into my underwear! I must've been overly enthusiastic when rearranging my wardrobe in the rest room, because instead of just tucking in my shirt, I had all but bared my bottom! To make matters worse, I was wearing "thigh highs." (For the uneducated hosiery shopper, "thigh highs" are like pantyhose in the form of really long socks, with a very tight elastic band to hold them up at the top of your leg.) They are best covered up, especially when standing brazenly in the hallway of one of the largest ministries in the free world!

Obviously, my friend had been staring off at the horizon

while we were contemplating God's sovereignty because he was traumatized by my exhibition. Here we were talking about holy and divine things, and I had flesh hanging out all over! I was desperate for a hole to crawl into!

MY EMBARRASSING INDECENT-EXPOSURE ESCAPADE IS A FITTING METAPHOR FOR THE REST OF MY LIFE.

My embarrassing indecent-exposure escapade is a fitting metaphor for the rest of my life. From the moment I gulped my first breath in a hospital delivery room in Central Florida to this very moment that I'm typing away, fueled by frequent sips of Diet Coke, I've had flesh showing. Born with a healthy body, I was also born with a healthy sin nature. As an infant, all I thought about was food and sleep—basically, getting my own needs met. And as you can imagine, narcissistic newborns grow up into egocentric adults. I'm a colorful sinner, and I've fallen woefully short of God's glory. I'm desperate for divine help. We all are.

C. S. Lewis paints a vivid description of how we humans seem to desecrate every good thing God does for us. In his book *Letters to Malcolm*, Lewis writes, "We poison the wine as He decants it into us; murder a melody He would play with us as the instrument. We caricature the self-portrait He would paint. Hence all sin, whatever else it is, is sacrilege."[1] The memory of exposed pantyhose may elicit a sheepish grin, but the sober reality of my own sacrilege causes me to shudder.

What about you? Do you ever shudder at the thought of your own sin? Do you feel desperate for God's mercy?

A Boy Named Bo

One of my favorite Old Testament stories about someone else who was desperate for mercy begins with a little boy who was saddled with a big name. He first appears in 2 Samuel 4:4:

> He was five years old when the news about Saul and Jonathan came from Jezreel. His nurse picked him up and fled, but as she hurried to leave, he fell and became crippled. His name was Mephibosheth.

This verse provokes more questions than it answers. Who was this poor boy who was dropped by his harried nurse and crippled as a result? Let's focus on his family tree for a minute or two and review his boyhood biography.

Mephibosheth was the son of Jonathan and the grandson of Saul, who was the first king of Israel. Mephibosheth's grandfather hated a guy named David (Jesse's boy whose shepherding skills led him to a face-off with a grouchy giant named Goliath). Saul got really mad when women greeted his army (after David had rocked Goliath's world!) by singing, "Saul has slain his thousands, and David his tens of thousands." David's soaring popularity put King Saul a distant second in the public opinion polls and left him seething with envy.

To complicate matters, David was also the best friend of

Saul's son Jonathan. The two loved to hunt and fish together, and they double-dated at the prom. (That's not an exact Hebrew translation!) The Bible says Jonathan loved David as he loved himself. Nonetheless, King Saul couldn't get past his own insecurity where David was concerned, and it poisoned him to the point that he decided to plot David's murder. But Jonathan defied his dad and helped David escape to the hills. (You can read 1 Samuel 20 for the rest of the story.)

Jonathan knew God had big plans for David and that He had anointed David to be the future king. So when Jonathan and David said their farewells, Jonathan looked David in the eye, and thinking of his future offspring who would likely live under David's rule, he asked David to promise him one thing: "Do not ever cut off your kindness from my family—not even when the LORD has cut off every one of David's enemies from the face of the earth" (1 Samuel 20:15). David gladly agreed to the request out of love for Jonathan.

Many years later, Saul and his army were defeated in a bloody battle with the feisty Philistines. Saul lost three of his sons, including Jonathan, and took his own life by falling on his sword—kind of a Hebrew hara-kiri. Afterward, the front page of the *Jerusalem News* reported that David was finally going to become the king of Israel. That news alarmed Saul's buddies and family members.

You see, in those days one of the first things a new king

did was to kill all the royal family members and others who were loyal to the previous king. This tradition tended to discourage anyone from plotting an overthrow of the new hierarchy! Of course, David had no intention of following that cruel tradition, but the few remaining relatives of Saul didn't know that. And they were especially worried about the safety of little Mephibosheth, because he had become the presumptive heir to the throne. Now here we are—finally back to the verse that started this whole soap opera of biblical history!

> He was five years old when the news about Saul and Jonathan came from Jezreel. His nurse picked him up and fled, but as she hurried to leave, he fell and became crippled. His name was Mephibosheth. (2 Samuel 4:4)

In other words, when the family hurried to escape, the nanny ran to get Mephibosheth from the royal playroom. But Bo didn't want to leave his Legos, so he tried to squirm out of the nanny's grasp, and she accidentally dropped him, breaking his ankles on the stone floor.

With little Mephibosheth whimpering in pain, they escaped to a place far away called Lo Debar, which in Hebrew means "barren place." Lo Debar was a little town lacking in orthopedic surgeons, so Bo's ankles didn't heal correctly, and he was permanently crippled in both feet. He moved into the home of one of his grandfather's friends and toiled away the years in obscurity—a crippled young man, forsaken in a foreign city.

Twenty years later there was a knock at the door, and a well-dressed official from Jerusalem told Mephibosheth to gather his things and follow him to the palace of King David. Can you imagine what Bo was thinking? He was probably scared to death, afraid that he'd be put to death for his family's transgressions. Why else would David summon a cripple who was the grandson of the mad king who tried to murder him?

> So King David had him brought from Lo Debar, from the house of Makir son of Ammiel.
> When Mephibosheth son of Jonathan, the son of Saul, came to David, he bowed down to pay him honor.
> David said, "Mephibosheth!"
> "Your servant," he replied. (2 Samuel 9:5–6)

I have so much in common with Mephibosheth. How about you? Have you spent most of your life running from the fact that you're crippled by sin?

If you're anything like me, you try to hide your crippled heart behind an elaborate curtain of Christian activity—as if "being good" will somehow lessen your desperate need for God's mercy. Or maybe, like Mephibosheth, your heart has become a barren place, and you often feel inadequate, undeserving, and unloved.

IF YOU'RE ANYTHING LIKE ME, YOU TRY TO HIDE YOUR CRIPPLED HEART BEHIND AN ELABORATE CURTAIN OF CHRISTIAN ACTIVITY.

Chapter 1: *Crippled by Sin*   9

Our Father's Acceptance

My parents divorced when I was five years old. It wasn't a friendly divorce like the ones depicted on television sitcoms; my parents weren't amicable. Like most children, I worried that their breakup was my fault. And I tried to be very, very good so that Dad would come back home and everyone would be happy again. But he didn't. He went to live with my new stepmother and stepbrother, and I got to visit them on weekends.

Dad usually called on Thursday nights to let me know what time he was going to pick me up the next day. Anticipating his arrival turned Fridays into red-letter days! I would be so excited about seeing him that I could hardly pay attention in school. As soon as the bell rang to end the school day, I'd race home and climb into the tree fort in the big oak in our backyard. From that perch I could see the road leading to our house. I would sit and watch the big stone gates that marked the entrance to our neighborhood, waiting for Daddy's truck to drive through.

When the time came for him to pick me up, I would stand up and stare intently at the gates, literally willing my father to drive through. Sometimes I'd stand there for hours waiting for him to drive up. And every now and then, Mom would have to come out in the yard and gently tell me to climb down from the tree because it was dark and dinner was ready.

My father didn't plan on forgetting me or breaking his promises. He never intended to hurt me. He was just torn between two families, torn between following God and following his own desires, and I got caught in the middle. But I didn't understand all that when I was in the first grade.

Mom remarried a man named John Angel a few years after the divorce. I liked him from the beginning because he laughed a lot and teased me, and he used to lift me up in the air by putting his hands under my elbows and hoisting me over his head like a barbell. (I'm still very impressed with men who can hoist me over their heads!) But I wasn't sure if John really loved me, because he was my *stepfather*.

One day, as John and I were walking through the mall together, we ran into two women who were teachers at a school where he had been a principal many years before. They exchanged pleasantries and were catching up on career changes when one of them looked down at me and exclaimed, "Oh, John, your little girl is so cute. She looks just like you!"

I can still remember stiffening when she said that, because I just knew he was going to say that I couldn't look like him because I wasn't his real daughter. My heart sank at the thought of having my stepchild status pointed out in the middle of the mall. But then God smiled at me through John's response.

He paused, looked down at me, and said, "She does look

like me, doesn't she?" Then he grinned and reached for my hand, saying firmly, "Yep, she's mine." And we walked away holding hands.

> "Don't be afraid," David said to him, "for I will surely show you kindness for the sake of your father Jonathan. I will restore to you all the land that belonged to your grandfather Saul, and you will always eat at my table."
> …So Mephibosheth ate at David's table like one of the king's sons.
> …And Mephibosheth lived in Jerusalem, because he always ate at the king's table, and he was crippled in both feet. (2 Samuel 9:7, 11, 13)

Mephibosheth expected punishment—even death—in David's court. The only prayer in his heart was for a political pardon. I expected to be labeled a stepchild. But we both found mercy. Instead of being disowned, we ate dinner. Instead of being punished, we got a room in the palace. Instead of being abandoned, we were adopted.

What about you? Have you ever expected to be disowned? Rejected?

Maybe you expect rejection from a perfect God because of your less-than-perfect past. Or maybe you're spiritually crippled by a sin that seems unforgivable. But the good news of the gospel is that our heavenly Father loves us with an everlasting love. We just need to be more like Jonathan's son in order to realize it.

We need to acknowledge the fact that we're crippled—that there is nothing righteous in us, that we are desperate for His mercy. And when the Spirit prompts us to recognize our need for salvation, God provides a Savior through the sacrifice of His only son, Jesus, who rescues us from barren places and gives us a seat next to Him at the Lord's banquet table.

Because of God's mercy, our stained hearts have been bleached by the blood of the Lamb. The God who spoke the universe into existence, who breathed life into Adam, who stretched out the heavens and the necks of giraffes, has looked down, taken our hand in His, and said, "Yep, she's Mine." Even though we're crippled, we have been royally adopted by the King of Kings and Lord of Lords. We are listed as His next of kin. Our names are written on His hands and in His book of life. His love for us is based on His character, not our performance. And it is greater than we could ever hope for or imagine.

> He himself bore our sins in his body on the tree, so that we might die to sins and live for righteousness; by his wounds you have been healed. (1 Peter 2:24)

Blessed are the desperate.

WE NEED TO ACKNOWLEDGE THE FACT THAT WE'RE CRIPPLED— THAT THERE IS NOTHING RIGHTEOUS IN US, THAT WE ARE DESPERATE FOR HIS MERCY.

Hopeful Reflections

1. What embarrassing motives in your heart have been exposed recently? _____

   _____

   _____

   _____

   _____

   _____

   _____

   _____

   _____

2. What do you think your response would have been if you were Mephibosheth and you were summoned to the king's palace? _____

   _____

   _____

   _____

   _____

   _____

   _____

   _____

   _____

   _____

   _____

3. Can you remember a time when you sensed God looking down with tenderness and mercy, taking your hand in His, and saying, "Yep, she's Mine"? _____

_____

_____

_____

_____

_____

_____

_____

_____

4. Read Ephesians 1:3–14. Read it again, out loud, and substitute your first name every time the word *us* appears (i.e., "God had adopted Lisa…"). _____

_____

_____

_____

_____

_____

_____

_____

_____

_____

_____

The glory of God hasn't really been
an all-absorbing passion in our lives and prayers.
How little we have lived in the likeness of the Son
and in sympathy with Him for God
and His glory alone.
Take time to allow the Holy Spirit
to reveal how deficient we have been in this.
True knowledge and confession
of sin are the sure path to deliverance.

—Andrew Murray
The Chief End of Prayer

TWO

Our Messy Lives

Fast-Forwarding through the Bad Parts

I've fallen head over heels in love with a strapping, blond, blue-eyed young man named Benjamin. He's athletic, brilliant, strong-willed, and he prays beautiful prayers. And he just recently finished potty training.

Benji is my best friend's three-year-old, and his shenanigans are a constant source of entertainment and inspiration. I went over to their house last week, and the minute I walked in the front door, I heard his husky preschool voice booming from the upstairs bathroom, "Mommy, I need you. I've made a *big* mess!" And in a flash, Kim was running up the stairs, two at a time. She's learned the hard way that sometimes even potty-trained toddlers can wreak havoc in the bathroom!

Sitting downstairs on their couch, I could hear Benji chattering enthusiastically about pirates while Kim cleaned up one of his daily debacles. Benji is supremely confident that his mom will help him when he makes a mess. He knows he would probably get a spanking if he made the mess on purpose, but his security stems from the fact that Kim has never left him alone in the aftermath of one of his creative demolition sprees.

I think most of us find it increasingly difficult to ask for help as we get older. It's cute for a three-year-old to need help with his messes, but it's not so cute for us as adults to admit we can't clean up after ourselves. So we end up stumbling through life, desperate for help but too afraid or embarrassed to admit it.

A friend of mine named Barbara told me another little-boy story about her youngest son, an energetic five-year-old named Buck. His three older brothers are school-age, so Buck has learned to entertain himself as he sits alone in the back of the van while Barbara drives to and from school, the grocery store, basketball practice, etc. Buck makes up stories and narrates them out loud while he's being chauffeured around town. His habit is even more precious because of his little-boy lisp.

> IT'S CUTE FOR A THREE-YEAR-OLD TO NEED HELP WITH HIS MESSES, BUT IT'S NOT SO CUTE FOR US AS ADULTS TO ADMIT WE CAN'T CLEAN UP AFTER OURSELVES.

A few weeks ago, Barbara noticed that Buck was making really strange sounds in the middle of one of his stories—kind of a cross between a squeak and a whir. She looked in the rearview mirror and said, "Buck, what are you doing, honey?" He looked up innocently and responded, "I'm just fast-fawadding thwoo the bad pawts, Momma."

I think one of the main reasons we have such a difficult time admitting our need for mercy is because we're too quick with the fast-forward button! We just don't want to acknowledge that we're sinful. I certainly don't like thinking about the ugly places in my heart and life. I'd much rather race past the bad parts and goggle at the good parts!

I was brought up in the South, where most of us are taught that it's bad manners to discuss anything distasteful. Fast-forwarding through the bad parts and ignoring messes is an art form we've perfected by the time we get our braces off! Cultural expectations and traditions form a sort of spiritual charm school where all students must look good on the outside and deny or disguise their need for help. It's socially unacceptable—tacky even—to be a sinner, and desperation is something that well-mannered people simply refuse to acknowledge. Pharisaism didn't disappear when Jerusalem fell; it just relocated to the land of antebellum homes and fried okra!

How about you? Are you a fast-forwarding female who denies her spiritual desperation?

A Pharisee in Denial

There's a familiar story in the Gospels about a stereotypical pew-warming Pharisee who read the Old Testament but didn't know the Author. When questioned by Jesus, he refused to admit that he was a sinner and tried to fast-forward through the bad parts of his life. He was an attorney—some lawyers are quite gifted at fast-forwarding past the facts!—and he was trying to trap Jesus at an intellectual intersection.

> On one occasion an expert in the law stood up to test Jesus. "Teacher," he asked, "what must I do to inherit eternal life?"
>
> "What is written in the Law?" he replied. "How do you read it?"
>
> He answered: "'Love the Lord your God with all your heart and with all your soul and with all your strength and with all your mind'; and, 'Love your neighbor as yourself.'"
>
> "You have answered correctly," Jesus replied. "Do this and you will live."
>
> But he wanted to justify himself, so he asked Jesus, "And who is my neighbor?" (Luke 10:25–29)

This lawyer was obviously a *summa cum laude* graduate of spiritual charm school! Notice how his pride reared its ugly head in his response to Jesus' statement about *doing* what the law commands. If he had been honest, he would've said, "I know what the law says, Jesus, but I can't possibly live it! I can't love God with all of my heart, soul, strength and mind. I've tried—really I have—but I just can't do it by myself. I'm a selfish nerd, and I have a tendency to cuss in traffic. Besides, I don't even *like* my neighbors, much less *love* them!" But instead of admitting his sin, the lawyer cleared his throat and asked the Prince of Peace a petty question. (It's important to note here that no matter how hard you try, you can't distract deity!)

Now if I were Jesus, I would've demanded contrition for his condescending cowardice. I would've put him in his place by pointing out his pride. Of course, my heart is filled with the same disease I despise in the grouchy guys of the Bible. As Paul, the reformed-murderer-turned-awesome-apostle, said, I'm the chief of all sinners. But it's so much easier to point out someone else's sin than to recognize the reprobate in the mirror.

> *How's your "heart-sight"? Do you see other people's sins more clearly than your own?*

Thank goodness our Savior is full of the mercy we're so desperate for! He must've seen something of value smoldering deep in this attorney's sanctimonious soul because He didn't snuff him out. Instead, He braced the bent reed of the man's heart with a wonderful story about grace:

> In reply Jesus said: "A man was going down from Jerusalem to Jericho, when he fell into the hands of robbers. They stripped him of his clothes, beat him and went away, leaving him half dead. A priest happened to be going down the same road, and when he saw the man, he passed by on the other side. So too, a

IT'S SO MUCH EASIER TO POINT OUT SOMEONE ELSE'S SIN THAN TO RECOGNIZE THE REPROBATE IN THE MIRROR.

Levite, when he came to the place and saw him, passed by on the other side. But a Samaritan, as he traveled, came where the man was; and when he saw him, he took pity on him. He went to him and bandaged his wounds, pouring on oil and wine. Then he put the man on his own donkey, took him to an inn and took care of him. The next day he took out two silver coins and gave them to the innkeeper. 'Look after him,' he said, 'and when I return, I will reimburse you for any extra expense you may have.'" (Luke 10:30–35)

Notice that Jesus said these people were traveling from Jerusalem to Jericho. In other words, the priest and the Levite were walking home after a long week at the "office." They had been busy working in the temple in downtown Jerusalem. The priest had been burning incense, offering sacrifices, and reciting prayers. He had presided over legal cases, and he had blessed babies. The Levite, who was subordinate to the priest in the holy hierarchy, also had been assisting in the traditions of temple worship. The two had been busy doing the work of the Lord—the very *public* work of the Lord. But now they were on their way home to the suburbs to rest. (Interestingly, the road they were walking was often referred to as "The Way of Blood" because it had such a bad reputation for criminal activity. Just imagine walking through an inner-city street after dark, and you'll get the picture.)

It is important to understand where the priest and the Levite had been and where they were going in order to see the application of this story to our everyday lives. A ceremonial law in the Old Testament (which these men revered) states that anyone who touches a dead body shall be rendered "unclean" for seven days. Some Bible teachers say that the priest and the Levite probably didn't stop to help the man in the ditch because they didn't want to become unclean in case he died in their arms. But the fact that Jesus said they were walking *from* Jerusalem *to* Jericho makes ritual purity a moot point. They were finished with their temple responsibilities and were headed home. They didn't have to worry about being ceremonially unclean because they weren't going to be performing any ceremonies in Jericho!

See, this dastardly duo prided themselves on keeping the *letter* of the law. They dotted their i's and crossed their t's and thought they had their spiritual bases covered. But their legalism didn't register on the righteousness Richter scale because they lacked love.

Engaging the Heart

Several years ago, one of my close friends complained to her husband that she wanted to spend more quality time with him. She was busy with their new baby, and he was busy starting up his law practice, so between diapers and depositions, they'd become ships passing in the night. He's a pragmatic guy, so he asked her exactly what she meant by more quality time. She told him she knew their lives were different now and they'd probably never have the amount of time alone that they used to; still, she wished that every now and then they'd spend twenty minutes or so in the evening just sitting on the porch swing and talking.

The very next evening, she was pleasantly surprised when he suggested that they go sit out on the porch after they'd washed the dishes and put the baby to bed. It was a beautiful night, and as they sat on the swing talking, my friend thought to herself, *Now this is wonderful. I feel almost like I did when we were on our honeymoon!* But then, right in the middle of her romantic remembrance, her husband lifted his arm from around her shoulders, looked at his watch, and said, "It's been twenty minutes. Are we OK now?"

He had fulfilled his obligation. He had crossed his marital t's and dotted his relational i's, but his heart wasn't in it. He had responded to the mechanics of her request, rather than the cry of her heart. Those of us who follow the rules without compassion might masquerade as spiritual giants in public, but we're pygmies deep down.

> THOSE OF US WHO FOLLOW THE RULES WITHOUT COMPASSION MIGHT MASQUERADE AS SPIRITUAL GIANTS IN PUBLIC, BUT WE'RE PYGMIES DEEP DOWN.

The priest and the Levite fulfilled their obligations, too, but only the Samaritan showed mercy. The fact that he was a *Samaritan* is an important part of the story. As you probably know, the Jews of that day despised the Samaritans. They wouldn't allow a Samaritan in their homes; doing so, they thought, would heap curses on their children. Their hatred for the Samaritans was so intense that they would slander them publicly in the synagogue and literally ask God to exclude them from eternal life.

All this prejudice was a result of a battle that took place 750 years before the time of Christ. The Assyrians had conquered the Northern Kingdom of Israel, otherwise known as Samaria. Their victory resulted in a country where Jews and Assyrians married and produced a race that was half-Jewish and half-Assyrian, or "Samaritan." Southern Jews were disgusted by these interracial marriages and considered the Samaritans a dirty race.

The battle lines deepened over the years. When the southern Jews returned to Jerusalem after their Babylonian captivity, they began to rebuild the temple. The Samaritans offered financial assistance, but the Jews said, "No thanks, you bunch of dirty half-breeds." So the Samaritans said, "Fine, you bunch of stuck-up nerds, we'll build our own temple on Mount Gerizim." (This isn't exactly a literal Hebrew translation either!) The Samaritans went on to establish their own priesthood. They took liberties with Jewish doctrine and basically disregarded everything the Jews held sacred.

In light of all this history, you would think that Jesus, being a Jew, would've made the Samaritan the bad guy—or at the very least, the guy in the ditch! But He made him the star. He silenced an uppity Jewish attorney by explaining the gospel of grace through a half-breed hero.

In this story of the Good Samaritan, Jesus taught Larry Law-Abider about mercy and his own need for it. He revealed to him that while we must have passion for God's law, we must also have compassion for people who need help. People just like him...people just like us. I bet that lawyer wished he'd been honest about his messy life from the beginning!

Have you been honest with God about the messes in your life? Or are you hanging on to outward appearances and following all the "rules"?

Our gracious heavenly Father entreats us to confess our mess. And to show us that it's OK to let down our pretenses, His Word is full of stories about unlikely people becoming heroes—a stuttering ex-con who leads God's people out of slavery; an unethical, little "IRS agent" who becomes a friend of Jesus; a sleazy woman whose testimony triggers a revival in her hometown. If you're embarrassed by your past, you're in good company!

IF YOU'RE EMBARRASSED BY YOUR PAST, YOU'RE IN GOOD COMPANY!

So be encouraged. When we humble ourselves, quit fast-forwarding past the bad parts, and admit that we're lost without Him, we become His unlikely children. Desperate, imperfect people...completely adored, accepted, and beloved by a perfect God.

Hopeful Reflections

1. When was the last time you ran to the Lord and said, "Father, I need You. I've made a big mess"? If it's been awhile, what mess do you need to confess right now?

_____

_____

_____

_____

_____

_____

_____

_____

_____

2. Would you characterize yourself as being more of a "law keeper" or a "lover of people"? Why?_____

_____

_____

_____

_____

_____

_____

_____

_____

_____

_____

_____

3. Are you more devout in public or in private? How do
    these two parts of your life differ?_____

    _____

    _____

    _____

    _____

    _____

    _____

    _____

    _____

    _____

4. What are the top ten reasons you need God's mercy?

    _____

    _____

    _____

    _____

    _____

    _____

    _____

    _____

    _____

    _____

    _____

    _____

5. Read John 3:16–21. Write down a list of the things you wish God would fast-forward past in your life. Pray for Him to forgive you of these things and cleanse your heart and mind. After praying, tear the list into small pieces and throw it away. _____

_____

_____

_____

_____

_____

_____

_____

_____

_____

$\mathcal{T}o$ forgive the incessant provocations
of daily life—to keep on forgiving
the bossy mother-in-law, the bullying husband,
the nagging wife, the selfish daughter,
the deceitful son—how can we do it?
Only, I think, by remembering where we stand,
by meaning our words when we say
in our prayers each night
"Forgive us our trespasses
as we forgive those that trespass against us."

—C. S. Lewis

THREE

Our Imperfect Pasts

Prodigals, Piña Coladas, and Bossy Big Brothers

A few months ago I was racing frantically around my house because I was late for a meeting and couldn't find my sunglasses. I have a hard time driving without them because my pupils don't dilate normally (a result of many summers spent as a squinty lifeguard!) and my eyes water a lot, even on cloudy days. I looked in all the normal places—in my purse, on the dining room table, on top of the dresser—but they were nowhere to be found. So with the clock ticking and my irritation level rising like the tide, I started looking in weird places, like inside the refrigerator and the washing machine.

Finally I decided to look under the bed. But when I got down on my hands and knees and pulled up the dust ruffle, I couldn't see anything in the darkness. It took me a few seconds to realize why it was so dark: I was wearing my sunglasses. They had been on my face the whole time!

It's pretty typical for me to be surprised by a spiritual truth in the same way I was ambushed by my Oakleys. I've heard lots of Bible stories since childhood. Many have been sitting in the hallway of my heart for years. But it often takes an "Aha!" moment for their truth to be wedged into the wrinkles of my soul. Those of us who've been Christians for a long time often become oblivious to the obvious.

Have you let the familiarity of Scripture dull the whisper of His Spirit in your heart?

The parable of the prodigal son is one of those familiar stories that has lost its punch for some of us. We've heard it a hundred times; we already know the end of the story. Many of us have even taught it a time or two. It's become a humdrum fable about a nice dad and his terrible teenager. But there are *two* sons in this story—the fallen young prodigal and the prideful older brother—and each boy reveals profound insights into our sinful nature. Most of us have probably played both roles at different times in our lives. I know I have.

> THOSE OF US WHO'VE BEEN CHRISTIANS FOR A LONG TIME OFTEN BECOME OBLIVIOUS TO THE OBVIOUS.

The Prodigal in Us All

I was a good girl when I was little. I obeyed my parents, did my homework, enjoyed going to church, and usually made my bed. I couldn't wait until dinnertime every night because our family sat around the table and talked, and I loved to regale everybody with my daily adventures! My chattiness often bugged my bright older sister because of my tendency to use really big words that I didn't understand. But her rolled eyes and numerous sighs didn't put a damper on my dinnertime routine; I was having way too much fun to be distracted!

However, when my teen years rolled around, all that changed. During the spring of my freshman year in high school, I had the rare and envied opportunity to join a clique of very popular junior and senior girls. I couldn't believe they wanted me—a lowly ninth-grader—to hang out with them! I quickly left my freshman friends in the dust of my newly found cool status. Almost as quickly, I also abandoned the standards and morals I'd been taught. Within a few weeks, I was drinking bottles of liquor from the stashes of the parents of my new friends. And since we didn't like the headaches that came with hangovers, we started smoking pot with our piña coladas.

My friends' parents never suspected that we were prodigals. We were from "good" families, we kept our grades up, and we stayed involved in lots of extracurricular activities. Boy, did we have them fooled! As a college friend of mine used to say, "We were as wild as Cooter Brown!" (I have no earthly idea who "Cooter Brown" is, but I'll bet he doesn't appreciate always being associated with delinquents!)

My parents, on the other hand, couldn't help but notice a change in my behavior. I had gone from being an outgoing, friendly, obedient daughter to a sullen, disrespectful young woman who didn't tell stories at dinner anymore. Dad Angel attributed my personality makeover to puberty. He thought my hormones had taken me hostage and I was just going through a typical teenage phase. But Mom, who has the discernment of the Minor Prophets, knew it was more than that. She knew my averted eyes and moodiness meant rebellion. I denied any wrongdoing and pled inno-cence, but Mom wasn't fooled. She prays too much to be hoodwinked by a teenage huckster.

She decided to send me away to a Christian camp for two weeks when the school year was over. I wasn't very happy about it; it certainly wasn't what my popular friends were doing over their summer vacation. The thought of spending two weeks in a musty cabin with a bunch of pasty, goody-two-shoes girls memorizing Bible verses sounded about as exciting as watching paint peel. So I argued and poked out my bottom lip and pouted with all the petulance I could muster. I should've won an Academy Award for my efforts, but Mom was immovable. She firmly believed God would woo my wandering heart at Lake Swan Camp.

Once I arrived, my resolve to hate camp lasted only a few hours. The other campers weren't pasty nerds, and we didn't just sit around memorizing Bible verses. There was a captivating speaker every night, and on the second night he talked about how true conversion brings about changed lives. He talked about what it meant to be a new creation in Christ and how we are supposed to live in such a way that other people see Jesus in us. I don't remember everything he said, but I do remember thinking that someone must've told him what I'd been doing back in Orlando. It felt like he was talking directly to me.

I couldn't get up the aisle fast enough. Somehow, the Lord gave me a glimpse of my dirty heart, and I knew—more than I'd ever known anything at fourteen—that I needed God to make me clean. I didn't understand the theological terminology; I didn't know His Spirit was *regenerating* my heart; I didn't know what *justification* meant. I just knew I'd made a mess of my life, and I prayed for Him to forgive me and take control. Another prodigal welcomed home!

Afterward I was so excited about Jesus that I couldn't sleep. I stayed up most of the night laughing and talking and praying with my counselor. We sat outside under a big tree and a full moon. I felt like Peter on the Mount of Transfiguration—I wanted to put up a shelter and stay at camp on that emotional and spiritual mountaintop. Besides, I was a little worried about going back down to the valley of reality and facing Mom. I knew I'd have to confess all the lies and rebellion, and I was afraid she was going to be really angry. I had gotten in big trouble a few months earlier for calling my little brother a bad name, and I knew that drinking alcohol and smoking marijuana were *so* much worse than that. Mom would probably want to send me to a convent or a juvenile-detention home.

I fretted about my certain punishment all the way home

from camp. But the minute the car pulled into our driveway, Mom came running outside and hugged me hard. I dissolved into tears and choked out the whole wretched story right there in front of the house. I waited for her rebuke, for stern words of discipline, or at least for disappointment. They never came. I don't even remember what she said. But I can remember exactly what she did. She smiled at me and put her hands on my cheeks and pulled me back into her arms for another hug.

> But while he was still a long way off, his father saw him and was filled with compassion for him; he ran to his son, threw his arms around him and kissed him. (Luke 15:20)

No matter how horrific our transgressions, we must always repent and return home. Our heavenly Father (along with a few earthly mothers) is lavish with His forgiveness. Jesus makes this point over and over again in the parables. Paul belabors the reality of reconciliation in his letters. And all but one of the apostles died for this hope—the hope and belief that God is an unconventional Father who runs toward us when we repent and pulls us into an everlasting embrace.

A Modern Parable

Philip Yancey wrote a poignant and powerful rendition of the prodigal's story—also highlighting the mercy of the dad—in his book *What's So Amazing about Grace?* I love the way Mr. Yancey puts this oh-so-familiar love story into a modern context we can relate to.

A young girl grows up on a cherry orchard just above Traverse City, Michigan. Her parents, a bit old-fashioned, tend to overreact to her nose ring, the music she listens to, and the length of her skirts. They ground her a few times, and she seethes inside. "I hate you!" she screams in an argument, and that night she acts on a plan she has mentally rehearsed scores of times. She runs away.

She has visited Detroit only once before, on a bus trip with her church youth group to watch the Tigers play. Because newspapers in Traverse City report in lurid detail the gangs, the drugs, and the violence in downtown Detroit, she concludes that it's probably the last place her parents will look for her. California, maybe, or Florida, but not Detroit.

Her second day there she meets a man who drives the biggest car she's ever seen. He offers her a ride, buys her lunch, arranges a place for her to stay. He gives her some pills that make her feel better than she's ever felt before. She was right all along, she decides: her parents were keeping her from all the fun.

The good life continues for a month, two months, a year. The man with the big car—she calls him "Boss"—teaches her a few things that men like. Since she's underage, men pay a premium for her. She lives in a penthouse, and orders room service whenever she wants. Occasionally she thinks about the folks back home, but their lives now seem so boring and provincial that she can hardly believe she grew up there.

She has a brief scare when she sees her picture printed on the back of a milk carton with the headline "Have you seen this child?" But by now she has blond

hair, and with all the makeup and body-piercing jewelry she wears, nobody would mistake her for a child.
Besides, most of her friends are runaways, and nobody
squeals in Detroit.

After a year the first sallow signs of illness appear,
and it amazes her how fast the boss turns mean. "These
days, we can't mess around," he growls, and before she
knows it she's out on the street without a penny to her
name. She still turns a couple of tricks a night, but
they don't pay much, and all the money goes to sup-
port her habit. When winter blows in she finds herself
sleeping on metal grates outside the big department
stores. "Sleeping" is the wrong word—a teenage girl at
night in downtown Detroit can never relax her guard.
Dark bands circle her eyes. Her cough worsens.

One night as she lies awake listening for footsteps,
all of a sudden everything about her life looks different. She no longer feels like a woman of the world.
She feels like a little girl, lost in a cold and frightening
city. She begins to whimper. Her pockets are empty
and she's hungry. She needs a fix. She pulls her legs
tight underneath her and shivers under the newspapers she's piled atop her coat. Something jolts a
synapse of memory and a single image fills her mind: of
May in Traverse City, when a million cherry trees
bloom at once, with her golden retriever dashing
through the rows and rows of blossomy trees in chase
of a tennis ball.

"God, why did I leave," she says to herself, and
pain stabs at her heart. "My dog back home eats better
than I do now." She's sobbing, and she knows in a flash
that more than anything else in the world she wants to
go home.

Three straight phone calls, three straight connections with the answering machine. She hangs up without leaving a message the first two times, but the third time she says, "Dad, Mom, it's me. I was wondering about maybe coming home. I'm catching a bus up your way, and it'll get there about midnight tomorrow. If you're not there, well, I guess I'll just stay on the bus until it hits Canada."

It takes about seven hours for a bus to make all the stops between Detroit and Traverse City, and during that time she realizes the flaws in her plan. What if her parents are out of town and miss the message? Shouldn't she have waited another day or so until she could talk to them? And even if they are home, they probably wrote her off as dead long ago. She should have given them some time to overcome the shock.

Her thoughts bounce back and forth between those worries and the speech she is preparing for her father. "Dad, I'm sorry. I know I was wrong. It's not your fault; it's all mine. Dad, can you forgive me?" She says the words over and over, her throat tightening even as she rehearses them. She hasn't apologized to anyone in years.

The bus has been driving with lights on since Bay City. Tiny snowflakes hit the pavement rubbed worn by thousands of tires, and the asphalt steams. She's forgotten how dark it gets at night out here. A deer darts across the road and the bus swerves. Every so often, a billboard. A sign posting the mileage to Traverse City.

When the bus finally rolls into the station, its air brakes hissing in protest, the driver announces in a crackly voice over the microphone, "Fifteen minutes, folks. That's all we have here." Fifteen minutes to decide her life. She checks herself in a compact mirror,

Chapter 3: *Our Imperfect Pasts*   39

smoothes her hair, and licks the lipstick off her teeth. She looks at the tobacco stains on her fingertips, and wonders if her parents will notice. If they're there.

She walks into the bus terminal not knowing what to expect. Not one of the thousand scenes that have played out in her mind prepare her for what she sees. There, in the concrete-walls-and-plastic-chairs bus terminal in Traverse City, Michigan, stands a group of forty brothers and sisters and great-aunts and uncles and cousins and a grandmother and great-grandmother to boot. They're all wearing goofy party hats and blowing noise-makers, and taped across the entire wall of the terminal is a computer-generated banner that reads "Welcome home!"

Out of the crowd of well-wishers breaks her dad. She stares out through the tears quivering in her eyes like hot mercury and begins the memorized speech, "Dad, I'm sorry. I know…"

He interrupts her. "Hush, child. We've got no time for that. No time for apologies. You'll be late for the party. A banquet's waiting for you at home."[1]

I cry every time I read that story. The young woman is painfully familiar. I've seen too many others just like her.

Have you seen a girl like her recently? Maybe hanging around the mall with a sullen face and a cigarette?

I saw a girl who reminded me of her today. She was behind the counter of a store in a small town in Alabama where I stopped for gas. She was probably about sixteen, but she looked younger. This particular prodigal was pale, petite, and ponytailed. And when she turned toward me to ring up my purchase, I was surprised to see that she was also very pregnant. Her left hand betrayed her status of unmarried soon-to-be mother. Her stomach got in the way when she reached out to hand me change, making her movements awkward and strained. Her girth seemed too big for her little body. And her eyes were so sad, as if the burden of her life was too heavy for her heart to bear.

EVEN OUR FEEBLE, FUMBLING REPENTANCE RELEASES AN AVALANCHE OF DIVINE FORGIVENESS.

I wanted to reach back across the counter, grab her hand, and tell her that even our feeble, fumbling repentance releases an avalanche of divine forgiveness. I wanted to tell her that our heavenly Father forgives little girls who have babies. I wanted her to know that God still looks at her with kindness and compassion even when others turn away in judgment and disgust. And I wanted her to know that the promise of God's redemption means her heart could be filled with hope again.

I smiled, trying to get her attention, but she turned away and ambled into a back room. I know I'll probably never even know her name, but I prayed for her for a long time as I drove down the dark interstate toward Tennessee. An old children's song came to mind with slightly different lyrics:

> Jesus loves the little children,
> All the children of the world.
> Young and pregnant, culture's blight;
> Still they're precious in his sight.
> Jesus loves the little children of the world.

Older Brothers

Let's not forget about the other character in Jesus' story. His sin ran just as deep as his wild sibling's, but its root lay in a heart hardened with pride.

> Meanwhile, the older son was in the field. When he came near the house, he heard music and dancing. So he called one of the servants and asked him what was going on. "Your brother has come," he replied, "and your father has killed the fattened calf because he has him back safe and sound."
>
> The older brother became angry and refused to go in. So his father went out and pleaded with him. But he answered his father, "Look! All these years I've been slaving for you and never disobeyed your orders. Yet you never gave me even a young goat so I could celebrate with my friends. But when this son of yours who has squandered your property with prostitutes comes home, you kill the fattened calf for him!" (Luke 15:25–30)

The older brother had forgotten about the hope afforded him because of his father's love. If his eyes had stayed on his dad's grace and mercy, they would've been wide with wonder. But instead he looked at his brother's crude condition, and he was filled with resentment. He begrudged his little brother's prodigal-no-more party because he thought *he* should be the guest of honor.

I was speaking at a retreat recently, and there was a woman in the front row who acted just like that older brother. She looked as if she had a bad case of indigestion, or else her girdle was way too tight! Her arms were crossed rigidly over her chest, and her mouth was set in a disapproving half-frown. I tried not to be distracted by her distress signals and turned my attention to the friendly faces in the room.

The theme of the message was God's call for us to be "grace-givers." I explained that we don't have the option to extend grace to some and withhold it from others (Luke 6:27–36). I emphasized His command for us to love each other and talked about how this love identifies us as lovers of *Him*. When I finished speaking, this sour-faced woman marched over to me and declared in a shrill voice, "Well, your message was very good. I sure hope *they*" (she gestured to a group of women whom she obviously thought were prolific prodigals) "were listening to what you had to say!"

Her arrogance left me speechless. I wanted to say, "Lady, you're the one who needed to hear that message!" This woman had a severe case of *Older-brotheritis*. Older-brotheritis is a nasty disease that strikes most Christians at some time or other. Symptoms include hardening of the heart; a jaundiced, judgmental spirit; and fever that burns with resentment when God gives mercy to someone you think is undeserving. This woman had all the symptoms!

> IT'S SO EASY TO SLIDE FROM THE POSITION OF YOUNGER BROTHER, WEEPING IN REPENTANCE, TO OLDER BROTHER, SMOLDERING WITH A SELF-RIGHTEOUS SENSE OF ENTITLEMENT.

We're all susceptible to this unforgiving fever if we forget our prodigal heritage. It's so easy to slide from the position of younger brother, weeping in repentance, to older brother, smoldering with a self-righteous sense of entitlement. But any pride we have regarding our position in Christ is preposterous. The only thing we've earned is severe judgment. Apart from God's mercy, the only thing we're entitled to is death.

Are you like the younger brother—far from home, wasted, and all alone? Or are you more like the elder son—full of pride, with a clouded memory of your own sinful past?

WE MUST KEEP IN TOUCH WITH THE HUMBLE GRATITUDE WE FELT WHEN WE FIRST RECEIVED HIS TERMS OF ENDEARMENT INSTEAD OF THE TERMS OF PUNISHMENT WE DESERVED.

The Scripture reminds us:

We all, like sheep, have gone astray, each of us has turned to his own way; and the LORD has laid on him the iniquity of us all. (Isaiah 53:6)

Whichever son we identify with, we're all desperate for God's mercy. We all live with imperfect pasts. But we have reason to rejoice: As believers in Christ, we're also the sons and daughters of a merciful Father who runs to draw us into His arms of love.

We must not forget what He has saved us from. We must keep in touch with the humble gratitude we felt when we first received His terms of endearment instead of the terms of punishment we deserved. We must never forget our desperate need for His mercy. And remembering, we will rejoice when He throws parties for other prodigals.

Hopeful Reflections

1. Do you identify more with the prodigal son or the older brother? Why? _____

   _____

   _____

   _____

   _____

   _____

   _____

   _____

   _____

2. Is your list of other people's sins more current than the one of your own trespasses against God? _____

   _____

   _____

   _____

   _____

   _____

   _____

   _____

   _____

   _____

   _____

   _____

3. Reread Luke 15:11–32. What is "slopping the pigs" a metaphor for in your life? _____

_____

_____

_____

_____

_____

_____

4. Make a list of three to five prodigals you know. Pray for their repentance and redemption. Consider praying daily for them for a month. Ask God to reveal what you have in common with each of the people on your list.

_____

_____

_____

_____

_____

_____

_____

_____

_____

_____

_____

_____

Finally he looked at me and said calmly,
"Who are you to think you are better than our Lord?
After all, he was singularly unsuccessful
with a great many people."
That remark, made to me many years ago,
has stood me in good stead, time and again.
I have to try, but I do not have to succeed.
Following Christ has nothing to do with success
as the world sees success. It has to do with love.

—Madeleine L'Engle

FOUR

Learning-Disabled Disciples

Mad Cows, Remedial Students,
and a Merciful Tutor

Soon after my parents' divorce, Dad bought a small ranch about thirty minutes outside of town. We had a motley menagerie of dogs, cats, horses, cows, chickens, and pigs on the ranch, along with forty acres to frolic in. For an all-American tomboy with dreams of becoming a veterinarian, it was paradise! Every weekend visit held the promise of new and exciting adventures. But my stepbrother, Ricky, wasn't quite as fond of our little house on the prairie as I was. He was more of a video-game guy than a Huckleberry Finn. That meant the task of coordinating all outdoor games and activities fell on my sturdy shoulders!

One of my favorite games was called "Trick the Cows." This stunt involved sneaking up on our herd of unsuspecting cows and shaking a coffee can full of feed. The coffee-can shake was their "dinner bell"—it was how Dad signaled for them to come to the barn. So when I shook it out in the pasture, the cows were tricked into thinking they were going to be fed. They would run toward me with an over-powering appetite for oats. I'd wait until they got really close then take off racing down a narrow path through the woods. My goal was to make it to the tree where Ricky was strad-dling a thick branch, watching me sprint narrowly ahead of the stampede. When I got to Ricky's perch, I jumped and swung up into the tree, out of harm and hoof's way! The only downfall to "Trick the Cows" was that they could only be fooled once or twice a day. Once they realized the ruse, they calmly went back to chewing cud no matter how vigor-ously I shook the feed can.

One Saturday, after the cows quit playing, I turned to a weary Ricky and said, "Hey, let's go try to trick the bull!" Ricky immediately objected that we weren't allowed near the bull—saying "the bull" with reverence and awe. I knew Ricky was right. Dad had made it very clear that we weren't supposed to go anywhere near the front pasture where he kept an ominous-looking Texas long-horned bull. This bull's horns were the width of a bicycle, and he looked like the cartoon bulls who blow smoke from flared nostrils when they're mad. Dad bought the bull to romance the girl cows, but this Romeo was too much of a bully to breed. Evidently, snorting and goring are not appealing attributes for a bovine beau because the cows ran away from Romeo every time he approached. He ended up quarantined alone behind barbed wire, waiting until Dad could sell him.

I assured Ricky that we wouldn't get too close to the

bull. My plan was to practice our "silent Indian walk" and sneak through the woods to the edge of the field where the bull usually grazed. He almost always stood on the far side of the field, so I thought we'd have a huge head start back to the fence. I promised Ricky that "Trick the Bull" was going to be the best game we'd ever played! He didn't look convinced and lagged far behind me as we heel-toed through the pine needles toward our prey.

But the bull was not on the far side of the pasture. As soon as I stepped out of the woods, I looked up to see him not more than twenty or thirty feet away—glaring at me. Evidently he wasn't pleased about being part of our afternoon fun because he lowered his head and snorted, preparing to charge. White-hot fear shot through me. I dropped the feed can and ran like the wind with the Texas killing machine thundering right behind me.

Somehow I managed to stay ahead of the bull through the woods, spurred on by twelve years of life flashing before my eyes. But as I streaked toward the fence, I realized I couldn't possibly take the time to stop and crawl through the barbed wire. I'd be trampled! So I ran toward a fence post, hoping I could jump on the strands of wire and then vault over to safety. I breathlessly jumped to the middle strand then hopped to the top strand, thinking I was home free. But then the U-shaped nail that held the barbed wire to the post popped loose, and I slipped and fell. As I slid down the post, one of the barbs sliced up the back of my leg

Chapter 4: *Learning-Disabled Disciples*   51

and got hung on my backside. I was skewered, like a marshmallow on a stick, with a bull butting me in the back. Dad heard our screams (Ricky was screaming too) and appeared within moments to hoist me off the fence before the bull butchered me.

I was a lucky little girl to escape with just a flawed fanny. If it hadn't been for Dad, the bull-busting hero, I would've ended up a shrieking shish-kebab! Most children probably would've tempered their daredevil deeds after such a harrowing experience, but not me. Soon after the bull brouhaha, I became infatuated with the feats of Evel Knievel and tried jumping over all kinds of things with a motorcycle, which of course led to many more bumps and bruises. Dad would shake his head and suppress a smile and tell me I was hardheaded. I just couldn't grasp the fact that I wasn't invincible. I was a pretty slow learner when it came to danger.

> I JUST COULDN'T GRASP THE FACT THAT I WASN'T INVINCIBLE. I WAS A PRETTY SLOW LEARNER WHEN IT CAME TO DANGER.

When We Think We Know Best

I think that's why I identify with Peter so much. Scripture exposes him as a fellow impetuous hardhead. And he was a real slow learner when it came to some simple spiritual truths, such as the fact that the Lord of the Universe—who created striped bass and belugas in the blink of His eye—knew more about fish than he did.

One day as Jesus was standing by the Lake of Gennesaret, with the people crowding around him and listening to the word of God, he saw at the water's edge two boats, left there by the fishermen, who were washing their nets. He got into one of the boats, the one belonging to Simon, and asked him to put out a little from shore. Then he sat down and taught the people from the boat.

When he had finished speaking, he said to Simon, "Put out into deep water, and let down the nets for a catch."

Simon answered, "Master, we've worked hard all night and haven't caught anything. But because you say so, I will let down the nets."

When they had done so, they caught such a large number of fish that their nets began to break. So they signaled their partners in the other boat to come and help them, and they came and filled both boats so full that they began to sink.

When Simon Peter saw this, he fell at Jesus' knees and said, "Go away from me, Lord; I am a sinful man!" (Luke 5:1–8)

Peter was an experienced fisherman. He'd sailed toward shore many times with a jaunty grin and a boat full of fish. He'd also pulled up to the dock with sunburned and sagging shoulders after a long day when he hadn't caught anything. This had been one of those times; they'd labored at their nets all night but pulled into port empty-handed and exhausted. Peter was probably glad to let Jesus use the prow of his boat as a pulpit; at least it'd be good for something. He stretched his legs and relaxed in the back of the boat, listening to the Rabbi teach.

Peter had met Jesus through his brother Andrew. Andrew had enthusiastically told him that Jesus was the Lamb of God—the one John the Baptist had talked about. And Peter had begun to think that Jesus was the Lamb of God, too, especially after He miraculously healed his mother-in-law. Jesus and some of the guys had come to his house for lunch after a synagogue service, but Peter told them they needed to go out to eat because his mother-in-law was sick in bed with a fever. Jesus brushed past Peter and went straight to the sick woman's bedside. When He gently touched her hand, she sat up in bed, completely well.

Now Peter smiled as the boat swayed, thinking of his mother-in-law's miraculous recovery and all the other special moments he and Andrew had shared with Jesus. They'd gone with Him to synagogues all over the region and listened while He taught. And although Peter had never considered himself much of a student, he was learning a lot from this radical Rabbi. But on this particular morning, when Jesus finished teaching and started handing out fishing tips, Peter's hardheaded ignorance was obvious:

> When he had finished speaking, he said to Simon, "Put out into deep water, and let down the nets for a catch."
> Simon answered, "Master, we've worked hard all night and haven't caught anything. But because you say so, I will let down the nets." (Luke 5:4–5)

You can almost hear the edge of exasperation in his voice. Sure, he believed Jesus was the Lamb of God and all that. But he didn't think Jesus knew a whole lot about fishing. That was Peter's forte. He'd been catching fish on Lake Gennesaret since he was a little boy. The water was his world! Peter was a pretty slow learner when it came to understanding that Jesus is in control of everything—that His forte is infinite.

PETER WAS A PRETTY SLOW LEARNER WHEN IT CAME TO UNDERSTANDING THAT JESUS IS IN CONTROL OF EVERYTHING— THAT HIS FORTE IS INFINITE.

Ten years ago I resigned from a job I adored. I was working for a youth ministry, and the job description fit me like a glove. Spending time with students, teaching Bible studies, and directing Christian athletic camps were my forte. I worked there for five years and thought I knew relational ministry the way Peter knew fish. But my boss and I had very different theological and philosophical perspectives. So when there was a financial shortfall, he said it would be a good time for me to look for another job. He told me I was a "square peg in a round hole."

I was devastated. I'd never been encouraged to leave a job before. Lots of arguments ran through my mind: *I'm a really hard worker, and the kids love me! His decision is biased and unfair!* I was so upset by the callous way he cast me off.

Fortunately I got a new job with a pharmaceutical company right away. And although I was thankful for the financial security, it just wasn't what I felt called to do. I didn't like developing relationships with people just to sell them something. I really missed full-time ministry, and I missed being with kids. So I prolonged my pity-party and woke up puffy-eyed and depressed for weeks. I told the Lord I didn't think He knew what He was doing. I told Him that although I believed He was the Lamb of God, I thought He'd forgotten me. He had a whole universe to run. How in the world could he keep track of the details in my life? How could He possibly know about the worries I had at work? I told God that my life was my forte, and I could do a better job running it than He could. I didn't think His plan was working.

Have you ever "raised your fist" to God, demanding control over the details in your life? Have you ever doubted that He really has your best interests at heart?

After Peter realized how dumb he was to doubt the Almighty's angling, he fell at Jesus' knees and cried, "Go away from me, Lord; I am a sinful man!" When his fog of faithlessness lifted, he knew he didn't even deserve to be in the same boat with Jesus. But Jesus didn't utter any harsh words of condemnation. He didn't even tell Peter he was hardheaded. He just told him he didn't have to be afraid. And He told him he was going to be changing jobs.

When my fog of faithlessness lifted, I

> HE HAD A WHOLE UNIVERSE TO RUN. HOW IN THE WORLD COULD HE KEEP TRACK OF THE DETAILS IN MY LIFE?

stopped crying tears of bitterness and started crying out to the Lord. And like His response to Peter, He didn't reprimand me with harsh words. In the middle of my misgivings, He gave me mercy. He told me to trust Him and not be frightened. I learned more from that difficult experience than from all my vocational victories. After sitting still at His knees, I finally realized that Jesus did a better job coordinating the activity of my life than I did. Even if I could, I wouldn't change the path I've taken since leaving youth ministry. Hindsight only highlights God's faithfulness. He's shown me that sometimes He quiets the storms in our lives, and sometimes He allows them to rage. But regardless of the weather, He always calms and comforts His children.

> SOMETIMES HE QUIETS THE STORMS IN OUR LIVES, AND SOMETIMES HE ALLOWS THEM TO RAGE. BUT REGARDLESS OF THE WEATHER, HE ALWAYS CALMS AND COMFORTS HIS CHILDREN.

Remedial Learners

Sadly, I'm still a slow learner when it comes to trusting God. And Peter was too.

Watching the Messiah find boatloads of fish in a stingy sea was mild compared to the other miracles Peter witnessed. He spent the better part of three years gaping at glory. He watched Jesus walk on water in the middle of the night, and he heard the wind obey His command. He was dumbfounded when a man born blind winked at him, and he stood transfixed when Lazarus walked out of his tomb trailing burial clothes. Of all people, Peter shouldn't have struggled with frail faith.

But the rock on whom Jesus said His church would be built was a painfully poky pupil. When the going got tough, Simon Peter blew it. He forgot the Messiah's messages and miracles, and he rejected Him three times before the cock crowed. He cowered in fear when Jesus was crucified. Peter failed with flying colors. Still, Jesus was merciful: Just a few days after Peter's denial, a resurrected Christ gave him a remedial lesson on the very same lake where it all started.

> Afterward Jesus appeared again to his disciples, by the Sea of Tiberias. [This is the name commonly used for the Sea of Galilee, also known as Lake Gennesaret.][1] It happened this way: Simon Peter, Thomas (called Didymus), Nathanael from Cana in Galilee, the sons of Zebedee, and two other disciples were together. "I'm going out to fish," Simon Peter told them, and they said, "We'll go with you." So they went out and got into the boat, but that night they caught nothing.
>
> Early in the morning, Jesus stood on the shore, but the disciples did not realize that it was Jesus.
>
> He called out to them, "Friends, haven't you any fish?"
>
> "No," they answered.
>
> He said, "Throw your net on the right side of the boat and you will find some." When they did, they

were unable to haul the net in because of the large number of fish.

Then the disciple whom Jesus loved said to Peter, "It is the Lord!" As soon as Simon Peter heard him say, "It is the Lord," he wrapped his outer garment around him (for he had taken it off) and jumped into the water. (John 21:1–7)

Once again Peter had been out fishing all night long on the very same lake and had returned with an empty ice chest. And once again, Jesus commanded a net-breaking catch, to Peter's utter amazement. You'd think Peter would've crouched low in the boat when John said it was Jesus on the shore. Hiding from God would've made sense with the bad taste of his own cowardly betrayal still fresh in Peter's mouth. But you've got to love his response, because instead of crouching, he leapt into the lake and began a furious freestyle toward Jesus. Impetuous Peter couldn't wait the few minutes it would take to row to shore!

Peter was indeed a very slow learner. Jesus had to repeat the exact same lesson at the end of their earthly relationship that He taught at the beginning. But Jesus tutored with such grace and mercy that Peter ran toward Him instead of running away.

How about you? Are there lessons God is having to repeat over and over in your life?

> JESUS TUTORED WITH SUCH GRACE AND MERCY THAT PETER RAN TOWARD HIM INSTEAD OF RUNNING AWAY.

Chapter 4: *Learning-Disabled Disciples*   59

When I was a baby believer, I learned that Jesus loves me and has my life in the palm of His hand. I learned to trust in the Lord and not lean on my own understanding. And I learned to put my hope in His faithfulness instead of my circumstances. But just like Peter, I'm slow. I'm still learning those same simple lessons. I hope the grooves cut in my heart by God's truth get deeper with each lesson I learn. Thank heaven we have such a patient and merciful Tutor!

Hopeful Reflections

1. Do you ever struggle with God's sovereignty and fight for control over the details of your life? _____

   _____

   _____

   _____

   _____

   _____

   _____

   _____

2. Make a list of the spiritual lessons you keep having to learn over and over again. _____

   _____

   _____

   _____

   _____

   _____

   _____

   _____

   _____

3. When was the last time you sensed God's mercy after making a big mistake? _____

   _____

   _____

   _____

   _____

_____

_____

4. Read 2 Corinthians 12:7–10. What lesson not yet
    learned is the biggest thorn in your flesh? _____

    _____

    _____

    _____

    _____

    _____

    _____

    _____

5. When was the last time you ran toward Jesus when you
    were wrong? _____

    _____

    _____

    _____

    _____

    _____

    _____

    _____

    _____

Part 2: *defined by grace*

We suffer the violation of indifference
on a daily basis, from friends, from family,
from complete strangers.
We think we've grown to accept it as part of life,
but the effect is building inside us.
We weren't made to be ignored.
And though we try to pretend it doesn't really matter,
the collective effect of living in a world apathetic
to our existence is doing damage to our souls.

—John Eldredge

FIVE

Relationships Aren't Enough

Looking for Love in Blind Dates and Buffet Bars

I'm thirty-six and single, and a *good* date comes along about as often as Ed McMahon and the Publisher's Clearinghouse truck! Fortunately (I think!), there are some very compassionate women who've taken up the torch of my "missing husband" as a worthy cause. And their interest in my matrimonial bliss has resulted in a flurry of blind dates.

My best friend Kim's mom, Michele Hill, is the leader of my hypothetical husband-search party. She called a few months ago to tell me she had not one but *two* blind dates lined up for me in Memphis (where she and the unsuspecting gentlemen live). So I quickly freed up a weekend in my calendar, Kim asked her husband to keep their boys for a few days, and we jumped into the car like two college girls bound for glory.

As soon as we arrived in Memphis, Kim and her mom set to work helping me choose exactly the right outfit, shoes, perfume, etc. for contestant number one. A blind date at thirty-six feels eerily reminiscent of the prom at seventeen! Thank goodness the baby blue tuxedos are safely locked away in the closet of our youth. But some of the butterflies are still there. *Will he like me? Will I like him?* Big sigh. "Just relax and have fun," Kim's mom said.

The first date was a perfect gentleman. And he taught me something about myself: I need better listening skills when the subject is the nuances of contractual law! Suffice it to say there were no fireworks—not even a sparkler.

Then came Saturday and my blind date with Hank. He had already called once to let me know where we were going and what I should wear, and he was adorable on the phone. He seemed witty and personable, and I thought, *Even if there are no fireworks, we're going to have a lot of fun!* Once again, Kim and Michele did my predate makeup and wardrobe consultation, and things were looking good. My hair was behaving like it was supposed to without any rebellious humps or curls. And I was wearing black slacks that have become known as my "magic pants" because they're quite flattering. Every single time I wear them, I get compliments. I have to admit I was feeling kind of cute waiting for Mr. Saturday Night!

As soon as Hank walked in the door, my hopes were confirmed. He had a broad smile and deep laugh lines, and he lit up the room with his authenticity and warmth. Within the first few hours, we discovered some remarkable similarities in our lives. We both had been on trips to Israel recently and had almost the exact same spiritual experience there. We'd even eaten at the same restaurants in downtown Jerusalem! We both had been scuba diving at the same dive site in Belize, Central America. And we were both competitive cyclists with the same brand of high-tech bikes. To top it off, he drove a truck just like my dad's, and it smelled like dogs because he's a veterinarian. That was completely charming to me because I had wanted to be a vet for years (until we had to dissect cats in high-school anatomy class, and my squeamish stomach debuted). Needless to say, the sparks were flying like the Fourth of July!

When we got back to Kim's parents' house at the end of our date, Hank walked me up to the door, and Kim's family invited us to join their rousing game of late-night Scrabble. Hank grinned and said he'd love to, while Kim and Michele stole bemused glances at me. Within minutes, he was telling stories about our similar adventures, and we were laughing and teasing each other as if we'd been dating forever. Of course, every time he looked down at his Scrabble tiles or turned around to refill his water glass, Kim and her mom would silently mouth things to me like, "He is so cute!" "You two are perfect together!" I have to admit I was having a hard time concealing my delight.

When Hank and I finally walked out to his truck to say good night, there was a beautiful full moon high in the sky. My magic pants were swaying in a gentle breeze, and I thought, *This has been the most perfect date in my whole life.*

Chapter 5: *Relationships Aren't Enough*   67

We talked a little more and made plans to go to church together the next day, and then he moved forward to hug me. As he was leaning down, I demurely reached up to put my hand on his shoulder. But when I did, the catch in my bracelet got tangled in the loose weave of my sweater and trapped my wrist to my chest. I flailed, desperately trying to free my "flipper hand" before he hugged me. But the more I wiggled, the tighter the bracelet became twisted, binding my wrist to my breast and trapping my hand in an upright position—kind of a little salute.

ALL RELATIONSHIPS
ARE INNATELY
FLAWED—BECAUSE
ALL PEOPLE ARE.

As Hank loomed in for the hug, I stiffened my flailing flipper so he wouldn't think I was a trashy girl who grabbed men's chests on the first date. After my shocking chest grope, he stepped back— I think a bit flustered by my flirtation—and said something polite like, "Thank you for a wonderful evening." I replied with a "thank you" of my own, all the while punctuating the night air with tiny birdlike circles from my wool-wrapped wrist!

Utopia Unmasked

When I turned and walked back up the steps toward the front door, I got so tickled by my predicament that I started laughing. Here I was, thinking I had finally discovered the illusive prize of blind-date nirvana only to be boondoggled by a bracelet! That night reminded me that no matter how hard we try, perfection really is just an illusion. Despite magic pants and passionate pyrotechnics, there aren't any perfect dates or marriages or friendships. All relationships are innately flawed—because all people are.

Have you ever been rejected in a relationship you thought was perfect? Have you ever been betrayed by a best friend or deeply disappointed in love?

IF WE ARE SOLELY DEFINED BY HOW OTHERS TREAT US, OUR SELF-ESTEEM WILL BE AS WOBBLY AS A NEWBORN CALF.

Some of us tend to ignore the fact that sin soils our species and remain diligent in our pursuit of relational bliss. In fact, most of us are defined by our quest toward the Holy Grail of perfect relationships. It's all but un-American to roll up the relational towel and walk off the court without a big W in the win/loss column. Surely if we just grit our teeth and try a little harder, we can create a perfect world where everyone gets along all the time. Right? Wrong. Friends part over petty disagreements, marriages melt down when moments of forgiveness are few and far between, and even the most noble communes collapse because someone didn't take their turn cleaning the bathroom. People aren't perfect. And if we are solely defined by how others treat us, our self-esteem will be as wobbly as a newborn calf.

That sober reality is juxtaposed against the fact that we were all created by God to be loved perfectly. *Agape* was the natural rhythm of the day in the Garden of Eden. God created Adam and Eve in His image and loved them perfectly. They, on the other hand, were supposed to worship Him with all their heart, soul, strength, and mind. It was a perfect relationship—that is, until Eve got deceived and ate some rotten fruit. Her mistake in menu choices separated the first man and woman from the only One who could ever love them perfectly.

Since Eve's initial apple craving, our appetites have continued to rock the love boat God ordained for us. In the wilderness the Israelites whined for meat instead of manna, totally disregarding God's merciful protection and provision. They begged for a buffet bar, forgetting that His presence with them in a cloud by day and a fire by night was infinitely more filling than bacon bits. The woman at the well just wanted a little Evian to get rid of her cotton mouth; she didn't realize the Gentle Stranger standing in front of her had the power to quench her thirst forever. And the crowds who followed Jesus after He fed five thousand people with a little boy's boxed lunch asked if He could turn a few more fish into feasts. They reminded our Messiah that Moses had provided manna in the desert, then they rudely asked what tricks He could perform:

> SINCE EVE'S INITIAL APPLE CRAVING, OUR APPETITES HAVE CONTINUED TO ROCK THE LOVE BOAT GOD ORDAINED FOR US.

Jesus said to them, "I tell you the truth, it is not Moses who has given you the bread from heaven, but it is my Father who gives you the true bread from heaven. For the bread of God is He who comes down from heaven and gives life to the world."

"Sir," they said, "from now on give us this bread."

Then Jesus declared, "I am the bread of life. He who comes to me will never go hungry, and he who believes in me will never be thirsty." (John 6:32–35)

In other words, Jesus is the only One who can satisfy our longings. All other relationships will fall short. No one else is able to completely satiate our hunger for perfect love. Every single person in our lives will disappoint us at some level. Some days they'll be busy when we need them to be still; other days they'll be self-centered when we need them to concentrate on us. Sometimes they'll bruise us with harsh words aimed right for the soft places in our soul. They won't meet all our emotional needs. They can't; they have too many needs of their own. They're sinners just like us. Only our Creator can love us perfectly, the way He created us to be loved. His love is the only thing that can define us without destroying us.

⌒ Have you opened up your heart and your life to God's perfect love?

Choosing to Trust God

The realization that our parents, husbands, friends, siblings, and children are mere amateurs at *agape* is a painful point to ponder. This world requires a lot of weeping once

Chapter 5: *Relationships Aren't Enough*   71

we recognize we're not going to be loved the way we long to be.

We've got two choices regarding what to do with the inevitable pain that results from this love liability. Our first choice is to avoid the pain at all costs—by far the most popular choice among women. It's amazing how spiritual this dance with denial can be! We smile our perkiest smile and say things like, "Just remember Romans 8:28. Everything will work out for the best!" That familiar verse in Romans has been misinterpreted more times than the federal tax code:

> And we know that in all things God works for the good of those who love him, who have been called according to his purpose. (Romans 8:28)

Yes, God will work out all things for the good of those who love Him, but the key phrase is "*according to His purpose*." Like it or not, sometimes His purposes can be painful!

Our second choice is to trust God with our pain. We need to remember another oft-quoted verse:

> The LORD is close to the brokenhearted and saves those who are crushed in spirit. (Psalm 34:18)

Do you think God would promise to be close to the brokenhearted if we weren't

DO YOU THINK GOD WOULD PROMISE TO BE CLOSE TO THE BROKENHEARTED IF WE WEREN'T EVER GOING TO SUFFER FROM BROKEN HEARTS?

ever going to suffer from broken hearts? He also promises He will count our tears and store them in a bottle (Psalm 56:8). Our heavenly Father is well acquainted with our bruised hearts and scabby relational knees. And He is not at all apathetic. Dr. Luke records a moment when Jesus was very affected by one woman's grief for her dead son:

> Soon afterward, Jesus went to a town called Nain, and his disciples and a large crowd went along with him. As he approached the town gate, a dead person was being carried out—the only son of his mother, and she was a widow. And a large crowd from the town was with her. When the Lord saw her, his heart went out to her and he said, "Don't cry." (Luke 7:11–13)

Then Jesus breathed the son full of life once more:

> Then he went up and touched the coffin, and those carrying it stood still. He said, "Young man, I say to you, get up!" The dead man sat up and began to talk, and Jesus gave him back to his mother. (Luke 7:14–15)

I picture Jesus smiling, His divine eyes swimming with tears, as He watched the woman's eyes grow wide with wonder as her son sat up in his coffin and said he wanted pizza for dinner!

Now I'm sure the widow's son wasn't perfect. Actually, he was probably a little spoiled because his daddy was dead and he was the only boy in the family. I bet his mom got mad more than once over his messy room. He was most likely a typical teen who didn't rise up and call his mom

Chapter 5: *Relationships Aren't Enough*   73

"blessed" every morning! Yet Dr. Luke tells us that when the Lord saw this mother, His heart went out to her. What an amazing thing that the Lord Himself is moved by our tears! He knows our disappointments. He winces when we aren't well loved. He holds us in our darkest hours, when life is anything but perfect and people don't meet the deep longings in the secret places of our souls.

My Mistake, His Mercy

I can't stop thinking about a phone call I received a few months ago. It was late in the afternoon when my secretary told me that a woman was calling to talk about a mistake I made at a particular Focus on the Family women's conference. My first reaction was to groan. There had been almost twenty thousand women at that conference, and I had already fielded a number of calls from grouchy women who hadn't liked their seats or parking spaces.

I was pleasantly surprised by a sweet voice at the other end of the phone line identifying the caller as Tracy. She told me that she'd been at the Nashville Renewing the Heart Conference and then asked if I remembered telling the audience I'd made a mistake while signing books there. I

> HE HOLDS US IN OUR DARKEST HOURS, WHEN LIFE IS ANYTHING BUT PERFECT AND PEOPLE DON'T MEET THE DEEP LONGINGS IN THE SECRET PLACES OF OUR SOULS.

grinned and told her I remembered that mistake very clearly.

I'd been hurriedly signing books during one of the conference breaks, writing over and over again the phrase, "He will never forget you," followed by the scripture reference, Isaiah 40:15–16. The reference somehow didn't seem right to me, but I didn't have my Bible with me and couldn't check it. I signed more than one hundred books in about forty-five minutes with this nagging suspicion that I was writing the wrong verse. Sure enough, as soon as I went back to my dressing room, I looked up the verses and was thoroughly embarrassed to read:

> Surely the nations are like a drop in a bucket; they are regarded as dust on the scales; he weighs the islands as though they were fine dust. Lebanon is not sufficient for altar fires, nor its animals enough for burnt offerings. (Isaiah 40:15–16)

Not exactly an encouraging inscription to write in someone's book! I quickly thumbed a few pages over in my Bible and found the passage I meant to reference:

> Can a mother forget the baby at her breast and have no compassion on the child she has borne? Though she may forget, I will not forget you! See, I have engraved you on the palms of my hands; your walls are ever before me. (Isaiah 49:15–16)

I figured that few women would actually look up the

scripture I had written in their books about dust and insufficient sacrifices. But I was afraid those few who did would be thoroughly confused! So when I walked back onstage, I told all twenty thousand women about my goofy mistake and read the pointless passage as well as the intended one. Then I told those who had a signed book to just change the zero in forty to a nine, and they'd have the correct reference!

After Tracy and I laughed over the phone about my big, fat *faux pas*, she said, "I called to tell you that your mistake wasn't really a mistake at all." She explained that early on the morning of the conference she had pretty much resigned herself to skipping the event altogether. Although she'd driven for several hours to get to Nashville, she felt so depressed that she didn't want to leave her hotel room. Just a few weeks earlier, she'd had a disturbing conversation with the doctor who treats her for cerebral palsy. He mentioned that her childhood medical records suggested she didn't receive adequate medical attention when she was born.

Tracy said that although she'd never had a great relationship with her mother, she couldn't imagine that her mom would have withheld medical treatment when she was a baby. So she called her mom and carefully broached the subject. Her mother got mad and basically told her that she hadn't wanted her when she was born, and she didn't want her now.

Tracy told me, "I just sat in my hotel room that morning and thought, *Why should I go to some Christian conference and believe a bunch of people telling me that God loves me, when my own mother doesn't?*" But she finally decided that since she'd driven a long way and had already paid the registration fee, she'd go ahead and attend.

EARTHLY RELATIONSHIPS AREN'T ENOUGH. IN THE END, THEY CANNOT SATISFY US COMPLETELY.

She'd been a Christian for a long time and thought she was familiar with most of the Bible. But she admitted, "When you came onstage and talked about your mistake and read those verses in Isaiah, it was the first time I'd ever heard them. And it was as if God Himself was standing in front of me saying, 'Tracy, I know your mother has forgotten you, but I will never forget you. I love you so much that I've engraved your name on My hands.'" It turned out to be one of the most meaningful moments in her life, and she thanked me for reading the verses that helped heal her broken heart. I'm convinced that God short-circuited my scripture memory for Tracy's sake!

Tracy knows what it feels like to be deeply disappointed in love. She bears the scars of a much-less-than-perfect relationship. The bruise of her mother's betrayal is still very tender. But she also knows what it feels like to be embraced by Emanuel. She's felt the compassionate caress of her Creator, and she's heard the whispered endearments of her heavenly Father. She's no longer defined by the meager mercy of her mom; she's defined by the perfect love poured out on her by the Prince of Peace. His amazing grace defines her, and she will never be the same again.

What about you? Are you defined by God's love, mercy, and grace or by the pain and disappointment you've experienced in the relationships of your life?

The same grace that defines Tracy can define us if we will give ourselves fully to our wonderful Savior. Earthly relationships aren't enough. In the end, they cannot satisfy us completely. Only God can love us with a perfect and everlasting love.

Hopeful Reflections

1. What are the main relationships in your life that you want to be perfect? _____

    _____

    _____

    _____

    _____

    _____

2. Do you remember what Abraham had to do with Isaac when their relationship came between him and God? Are there any relationships in your life that you need to figuratively place on the altar in order to put God back on the throne? _____

    _____

    _____

    _____

    _____

    _____

    _____

    _____

3. In what specific and personal ways has Jesus loved you perfectly?_____

    _____

    _____

    _____

    _____

_____

_____

4. What three adjectives best describe your feelings of being pursued, found, and loved perfectly by the Creator of the Universe? _____

_____

_____

_____

_____

_____

_____

5. Read Zephaniah 3:17. Try to spend at least twenty minutes alone thinking about the words you long to hear God sing to you. Write them down. Are they words of comfort? Forgiveness? Delight? _____

_____

_____

_____

_____

_____

_____

True quietness of heart

therefore is gotten by resisting our passions,

not by obeying them.

—Thomas á Kempis

SIX

The Money Pit

Trinkets or Treasures?

Several years ago I met a wealthy woman who reminded me not to be too affected by money. It was summertime, and I was in Texas on a business trip, staying in a very nice hotel. I decided to get in a quick workout in the hotel fitness center because I'd gained weight, and if I didn't lose a few pounds fast, the clothes I'd packed for the trip were going to cut off my circulation. I had literally gotten too big for my britches! So I pedaled the Lifecycle and stomped on the Stairmaster with reckless abandon. Soon I was exhausted enough to delude myself into believing I was but a fraction of my former self.

Sweaty but surely svelte, I waited for the elevator so I could go back up to my room and get ready for a banquet that evening. The elevator doors opened to reveal an impeccably dressed woman, dripping with elegance and gold jewelry. Her suit was beautiful, and her hair—like everything else in Texas—was big. (Luckily I'm not a smoker, because one lit match and the hair spray in that elevator would've blown up the hotel.) We were the only people on the elevator, and I noticed we were going to the same floor. I thought, *We're both women…we're staying on the same floor…we're bonded!*

I leaned toward her to begin a friendly conversation; I think I commented about the weather. She stared straight ahead, completely ignoring me. I thought, *Poor thing, she must be hard of hearing.* So I leaned in a little closer and repeated my comment a lot louder. This time she glanced irritably out of the corner of her eye and exhaled very loudly, as if to say, "You are sweaty and stinky and do not deserve my attention or my company." Flustered and embarrassed, I spent the next several minutes feigning fascination at the way the floor numbers lit up on the elevator panel. When the doors finally opened on our floor, the woman brushed past me haughtily and walked away without so much as a backward glance. I shuffled wearily to my room, feeling very out of place in such a posh hotel.

An hour or so later, I was showered, suited, and bejeweled myself (albeit with smaller hair) because I was hosting a formal banquet on behalf of a national ministry. The hotel banquet room was full of wealthy donors, and guess who was there in all her glory? My condescending elevator comrade! When the program was over, she sashayed across the room to me and gushed (with a melodramatic Scarlett O'Hara accent), "Eye wee-ush you had told me who you wah on the elah-vatah...eye would have luh-uved to have tah-alked to you...if only eye'd known who you wah!"

Apparently I was unworthy of this woman's good graces when I was just a chatty, sweaty nobody who obviously couldn't afford to stay in a fine hotel. But my Superman-like transformation into a poised performer clad in a DKNY suit and designer pumps caused her to reconsider. I could see her mental wheels turning, wondering if I was worthy of her conversation after all. Bertha Big-Hair probably plays perception Ping-Pong on a regular basis because her approval of others is tied to blue blood and bank accounts. She'll write a check for the underprivileged, but she'd rather they not check into the same hotel!

Have you ever given someone the cold shoulder because he or she was financially poor? Ignored someone's need because you felt that person was "beneath" you?

It's no wonder Hebrews tells us to keep our lives free from the love of money (Hebrews 13:5). According to Paul, loving money is the root of all kinds of evil (1 Timothy 6:10), linked inexorably with boasting, pride, abuse, and ungratefulness (2 Timothy 3:2). When our lives are defined by the love of money—ours or someone else's—we put gold

> BIG HOMES AND LAVISH LIFESTYLES MIGHT MAKE US THE ENVY OF OUR NEIGHBORS, BUT WEALTH DOESN'T GIVE US WORTH.

instead of God on the throne of our lives. Big homes and lavish lifestyles might make us the envy of our neighbors, but wealth doesn't give us worth. And big paychecks can't buy peace.

Besides, being defined by riches leaves us vulnerable to being robbed. Every stock market fluctuation or new car in the neighbor's driveway has the power to shoplift our security. We become lured into the land of plenty and become obsessed with having more. When the hope in our hearts is balanced on a dime, we're never really secure. We know material wealth can always be taken away from us, so we hang on to our stuff with a white-knuckled death grip.

He Could've Been a Millionaire

There's a sad story in the Gospels about a man who couldn't pry his fingers off his pennies—not even when he was presented with incomparable riches.

> As Jesus started on his way, a man ran up to him and fell on his knees before him. "Good Teacher," he asked, "what must I do to inherit eternal life?"
>
> "Why do you call me good?" Jesus answered. "No one is good—except God alone. You know the commandments: 'Do not murder, do not commit adultery, do not steal, do not give false testimony, do not defraud, honor your father and mother.'"
>
> "Teacher," he declared, "all these I have kept since I was a boy."
>
> Jesus looked at him and loved him. "One thing you lack," he said. "Go, sell everything you have and

give to the poor, and you will have treasure in heaven. Then come, follow me."

At this the man's face fell. He went away sad, because he had great wealth.

Jesus looked around and said to his disciples, "How hard it is for the rich to enter the kingdom of God!" (Mark 10:17–23)

HE WAS PROMISED THE TREASURES OF HEAVEN, BUT HE COULDN'T LET GO OF A FEW TRIVIAL TRINKETS.

The rich young man was offered the glorious opportunity to become a son of the God who owns the cattle on a thousand hills. But instead he settled for a condo in a gated community in Judea because he just couldn't part with his 401K. He was promised the treasures of heaven, but he couldn't let go of a few trivial trinkets. His sad story illustrates the most dangerous thing about loving money: It has the power to displace our desire for God.

What trinkets are you settling for? Are they really worth more than a relationship with the living God?

It's Hard to Let Go

Several years ago I went on a camping and climbing trip in the Sierra Nevada Mountains in northern California near Yosemite National Park. I was really excited about the trip because I love the outdoors and was looking forward to rock climbing for the first time. But the trip turned out to be much more than I bargained for!

Our campsite was literally forty miles off the beaten path. We drove up steep, winding roads for more than an hour—which caused several people in our group to hang their heads out of the van windows with symptoms that looked like seasickness. Then we stumbled out of the vans like drunken sailors into a clearing in the wilderness and hoisted forty-pound backpacks loaded with all of our gear (including a portable potty chair). We were not allowed to bring deodorant, shampoo, or any other scented supplies because we were told they tend to attract bears. But I'm kind of picky about hygiene, so I squirreled away a little deodorant stick and some shampoo, deciding I'd rather be risky than stinky!

Finally, after huffing and puffing uphill for miles, we made it to our campsite on a sheer mountain face. After gobbling some food that looked like potpourri, we promptly fell asleep under the stars (no tents were allowed on this trip) and dreamed about climbing the huge rock walls we'd hiked past all afternoon.

Early the next morning we gathered around our climbing instructors to learn the skills we would need to climb safely. We learned how to tie the ropes and strap into our harnesses, then we practiced the verbal signals we'd use when climbing in dangerous terrain. After an hour or so, I was ready for the tedious explanations and instructions to end. I wanted to start climbing—not just talk about it! So when the instructors said the experienced climbers could hit the wall, I bolted from the group even though, technically, I didn't have any previous climbing experience.

I quickly strapped on my harness—hoping it didn't magnify my fanny too much—and walked toward a giant granite wall reserved for advanced climbers. I'm pretty athletic and not afraid of heights, so I thought I'd have no problem with the climb. And I didn't for the first hundred feet or so. As a matter of fact, I was doing so well that a small crowd of admirers gathered at the base. Every now and then they'd shout out something encouraging like, "Way to go, Lisa!" or "Great move. You're a pro!" I was feeling proud, just brimming with confidence. But then I got to a ledge that arched out over my head. There was no way around it, and the only way up was to climb across it—which left me clinging to the wall, almost inverted, with the ground more than one hundred feet below.

My fans, still unaware of my beginner status, began to sense my fear. I guess anyone watching would've sensed my fear because I was white as a ghost, clinging desperately to handholds the size of stereo knobs and mouthing promises about going to the mission field in Africa if only God would let me live. The climbing instructors started yelling for me to let go of the handholds and simply hang on to the climbing rope. This sounded about as reasonable as telling someone, "Just step out of the plane because we'll throw the parachute out right behind you!" I was born at night, but it wasn't last night!

Somewhere deep in the recesses of my panicked mind, I knew that an experienced climbing guide above me—whom

I couldn't see—was holding on to the rope attached to my harness. I also knew that the rope would hold my weight and keep me from plummeting to the ground. But I couldn't think logically; I was too afraid of becoming a human pancake. I just couldn't let go of those wee handholds. So I clung there, sweaty and trembling, listening to the voices of the instructors below me become more calm and condescending—as if they were dealing with a strong-willed toddler who was refusing to let go of her blanket. They had the perspective and the experience to know that the petite protrusions I was gripping weren't nearly as secure as the rope I was tied to. They knew that all I had to do was let go of the rock and trust the rope, and I'd be safe.

When the muscle spasms started, I finally realized I couldn't hang on any longer. I was going to have to trust the rope. My stomach lurched when I let go, preparing itself for my demise. But I didn't become a climbing statistic after all; the rope held, and I dangled from the mountain like a kid in a park swing!

I was so thankful to be alive that I scrambled to the top of the mountain as soon as they pulled me over the ledge.

> IT'S SO FOOLISH TO HANG ON TO DOLLARS INSTEAD OF GOD'S DELIGHT IN US.

The sky never looked so blue, the air never smelled so sweet, and *terra firma* never felt so terrific! It was all I could do not to jump into the instructor's arms and sob with relief. I resisted, however, hoping to recover a few shreds of dignity. Later when I rappelled to the bottom of the mountain and looked up at the route I'd just climbed, it was obvious the rope was secure. My fear seemed foolish from that viewpoint.

It's so foolish to hang on to dollars instead of God's delight in us. The trinkets we cling to are tiny compared to the treasure we have in His grace. Worldly things make insecure handholds; they can always slip through our fingers. Our possessions may define us momentarily as wealthy, but they will eventually fade, spoil, and rust, leaving us paupers.

God's love is the only security we should cling to—the only rope that can keep us from falling into the money trap of pride and ungratefulness. So let's loosen our grip on our stuff and grab hold of God! Only His grace makes us truly rich.

> WORLDLY THINGS MAKE INSECURE HANDHOLDS; THEY CAN ALWAYS SLIP THROUGH OUR FINGERS.

Hopeful Reflections

1. Are you satisfied with your material possessions (home, furniture, car, clothes, etc.)?_____

_____

_____

_____

_____

_____

2. How often do you find yourself dreaming about earthly treasures (new home, new furniture, new car, new clothes)? _____

_____

_____

_____

_____

3. Read Matthew 13:44–46. Did you *stumble* upon the treasure of your salvation like the man in the field, or were you saved after a long *search* (going to Bible studies, church services, evangelistic outreaches, etc.) similar to the merchant's search for the perfect pearl?_____

_____

_____

_____

_____

_____

_____

4. What did the man in the field and the merchant do when they found their treasure?_____

_____

_____

_____

_____

_____

_____

5. Are there any trinkets you need to let go of in order to fully claim the treasure of an intimate, loving relation-ship with Jesus Christ? _____

_____

_____

_____

_____

_____

_____

_____

$\mathscr{A}$ real Christian is an odd number, anyway.

He feels supreme love for One whom he has never seen;

talks familiarly every day to Someone he cannot see;

expects to go to heaven on the virtue of Another;

empties himself in order to be full;

admits he is wrong so he can be declared right;

goes down in order to get up;

is strongest when he is weakest;

richest when he is poorest;

and happiest when he feels the worst.

He dies so he can live; forsakes in order to have;

gives away so he can keep; sees the invisible;

hears the inaudible;

and knows that which passeth knowledge.

—A. W. Tozer

SEVEN

Our Ridiculous Reputations

Touching Tassels, Embracing Emmanuel

At the end of my junior year in high school I was elected into an elite secret society called The Tribe. Only a few upperclassmen were initiated in a solemn ceremony, which ended with war paint and the presentation of personalized tribal headbands woven in orange and black, our school colors. (I can't tell you anything else about the ceremony, or I'll have to kill you!) Supposedly only the best and the brightest were inducted into The Tribe, so those headbands were symbolic of good students, great athletes, and strong leaders. A headband around your rearview mirror (the most noticeable place you could put it without looking too conspicuous) meant you were one of the "chosen few," with a bright future and a popular reputation. We were happy to be identified by those headbands because our reputations—the way others perceived us—meant so much to us. Our reputations defined us.

One of the deepest theologians I've ever met was never defined as having a bright future and a popular reputation.

She was a high school classmate who never made it into The Tribe. Her name is Leigh, and she lived across town in a trailer park. Her parents worked at the bowling alley; the rumor was that they were both alcoholics. I'm not sure about that. But they were poor, and it was obvious. Leigh wore polyester before Austin Powers brought it back in style. She was in remedial classes and had a speech impediment. She wasn't a scholar or a leader. Not only did she not have an orange-and-black headband hanging from her rearview mirror; she didn't even drive a car.

We got to know each other through an organization called the Fellowship of Christian Athletes (an evangelical, nondenominational "youth group" that involves all of the interested athletes in school). Leigh wasn't an athlete, but she loved Jesus and she loved to socialize; therefore she assumed she was a perfect candidate for the *Fellowship* and *Christian* parts of FCA.

I was the president of FCA my senior year, and driving Leigh to and from meetings was my responsibility. She was usually standing in the road grinning when I drove up; I think FCA meetings were the highlight of her week. She loved to sing and listen to the speakers, and she gleefully joined in with whatever silly activity was planned (i.e., who could stuff the most marshmallows in his or her mouth and still say "chubby bunny" coherently).

One night when we were driving to a meeting, Leigh

asked me for a favor. She said she really wanted to sing a solo for the group and wondered if that would be okay. I didn't know what to do. Leigh didn't have a very good voice, and I was afraid the other kids would make fun of her. Some of them already considered her a misfit in our "cool" Christian club. But I just couldn't say no—not when she was so excited about it.

CARNEGIE HALL WOULD BE HARD-PRESSED TO COME UP WITH A MASTERPIECE THAT COMPARES WITH LEIGH'S SIMPLE SOLO.

I was nervous when she stood up to sing. And sure enough, as soon as the first off-key notes echoed through the room, some of the kids started to giggle. But Leigh didn't seem to notice. Popularity was never a passion of hers. She stood perfectly still with her shoulders square, her back straight, and her eyes closed. And she smiled almost dreamily while she sang:

Some-ting bootiful, Some-ting good,
All my confooshun, He undurstood.
All I had to offah Him was bwokin-ness and stwife,
But He made some-ting bootiful of my life.

Then she opened her eyes, smiled a big, wide, innocent smile that illuminated the entire room, and slowly sat down. The football players had stopped giggling, and we all had stopped wiggling. Everyone in the room just stared at Leigh. Somehow we knew we had just witnessed a miracle. Carnegie Hall would be hard-pressed to come up with a masterpiece that compares with Leigh's simple solo. She might've struggled with Greek and grammar, but she completely understood the grace of the gospel.

She grasped—in a way that few of us ever do—the profound truth that our salvation is a gift we can't possibly afford. And she was delighted with the Giver. Reputation didn't matter to Leigh. She knew the only way she could go from rags to riches was through the mercy and forgiveness of Jesus Christ. And He transformed her polyester rags into white linen robes of righteousness. She didn't need to be identified by a silly headband; she didn't need to belong to a tribe. She was royally defined by the amazing grace of God.

I haven't seen Leigh in more than ten years, but I think about her often. Her testimony continues to teach me in gentle whispers. I'm continually challenged and humbled by the memory of her childlike faith. Leigh approached the banquet table of God's grace with empty hands; I've usually got mine full of Tupperware. I carry all my works of righteousness—Bible studies, Scripture memory verses, homeless shelter visits—toward His throne in spill-proof, microwave-able plastic. As if all the underlined passages in my Bible will add up like frequent flyer miles!

WE ARE SAVED BY GRACE, NOT BY WORKS. THEREFORE WE SHOULD BE DEFINED BY HIS GRACE, NOT BY OUR REPUTATIONS.

How about you? Are you depending on your reputation to define you before God and others? Do you have any spiritual "Tupperware" that needs cleaning out?

Somewhere in my silly, self-righteous soul, I harbor the mistaken belief that my sterling spiritual reputation must mean something in God's everlasting reward system. But Leigh's story reminds me that my reputation means absolutely nothing—that all those works of righteousness I have neatly stored up are worth less than the rags I wash the car with. We are saved by grace, not by works. Therefore we should be defined by His grace, not by our reputations.

Touching Tassels Instead of Toting Tupperware

One of my favorite stories in the Gospels is about a woman of no reputation who went from rags to riches. Her transformation took place at the hand of the same Messiah who made something beautiful of my sweet friend, Leigh. Her story is told in the Gospel of Mark:

> When Jesus had again crossed over by boat to the other side of the lake, a large crowd gathered around him while he was by the lake. Then one of the synagogue rulers, named Jairus, came there. Seeing Jesus, he fell at his feet and pleaded earnestly with him, "My little daughter is dying. Please come and put your hands on her so that she will be healed and live." So Jesus went with him.
>
> A large crowd followed and pressed around him. And a woman was there who had been subject to bleeding for twelve years. She had suffered a great deal under the care of many doctors and had spent all she

had, yet instead of getting better she grew worse. When she heard about Jesus, she came up behind him in the crowd and touched his cloak, because she thought, "If I just touch his clothes, I will be healed." Immediately her bleeding stopped and she felt in her body that she was freed from her suffering.

At once Jesus realized that power had gone out from him. He turned around in the crowd and asked, "Who touched my clothes?"

"You see the people crowding against you," his disciples answered, "and yet you can ask, 'Who touched me?'"

But Jesus kept looking around to see who had done it. Then the woman, knowing what had happened to her, came and fell at his feet and, trembling with fear, told him the whole truth. He said to her, "Daughter, your faith has healed you. Go in peace and be freed from your suffering." (Mark 5:21–34)

OK, let's do a quick scripture synopsis. Jesus was on His way to heal a really important man's daughter. Remember that during the time of Christ, a synagogue ruler was also a powerful political leader. So basically Jesus was headed to the governor's mansion with a big crowd following Him when He got sidetracked in the inner city. Suddenly He felt a surge of power sizzle through His sacred synapses. He stopped in His tracks and asked His disciples who touched Him. They were hot, thirsty, and claustrophobic, and they testily told Jesus that they had no idea who touched Him because there were a million people milling around. (I took a bit of liberty with the original Greek, but that's close!)

Mark tells us the woman who touched Jesus had been bleeding for twelve years, and most theologians agree that the blood flow was constant. His eyewitness account also tells us that she'd suffered a lot at the local HMO, spending all the money she had on treatments that didn't work. Dr. Luke leaves that little bit of medical malpractice out of his Gospel account (Luke 8:43–48), but Mark chooses to enlighten us about her derelict doctors! (In Luke's defense, Scripture does call her condition incurable.) The bottom line is that this woman was really sick, and she'd had to file Chapter 11 because of her overwhelming medical expenses.

We can also accurately say that she had lost her family and friends because the nature of her disease—constant bleeding—rendered her ceremonially unclean according to Jewish law (Leviticus 15:25–27). She wasn't allowed to darken the door of the neighborhood synagogue—a suspension that was more serious than most of us realize because back then a synagogue wasn't just for Saturday worship services; it was also the center of community activity.[1] The synagogue was where women met for Weight Watchers and Creative Memories and men gathered for chess and checkers. In other words, this woman was ostracized from the very heart of her community!

This loss of health, wealth, and relationships had left her reputation in tatters, making her an object of scorn in her neighborhood. Jewish culture assumed that prolonged physical problems indicated a big Pandora's box of unconfessed sin. The other women in town probably talked about her behind her back, trying to imagine the depths of her depravity. And over the years her heart was wounded again and again by these gossipy girlfriends and obdurate ob-gyns.

Have you ever felt ostracized or rejected by friends, family, coworkers? Have you ever been hurt by gossip—or hurt someone else because of things you said behind her back?

But then one day this woman looked up and saw the Prince of Peace walking through a parade of people. Here she was, a woman of no reputation, without wealth or stature to impress the King of Kings. She didn't even have a decent home to invite Him to for coffee. But she had faith. And she thought, *If I could just touch the edge of His robe, I know I'd be healed.*

She scurried quickly toward the crowd surrounding Jesus and then elbowed her way through to the front. She finally reached a place on the curb where Jesus would walk right past her. I like to imagine her waiting until Jesus got within reach and then stretching her hand out to touch one of the tassels hanging from the corners of His robe. The Bible doesn't tell us exactly how she touched Him, but it does tell us she was healed

IT CERTAINLY WASN'T TOO FANTASTIC A FEAT FOR HIM TO KNOW WHOSE HAND HAD BRUSHED HIS ROBE IN AN ACT OF DESPERATE FAITH.

immediately. Her hemorrhage halted the instant she touched His garment.

That's when Jesus asked who touched Him. Now, God wasn't confused, and He certainly isn't ignorant. He knows the number of hairs on our heads and the thoughts we're thinking at this very moment. So it certainly wasn't too fantastic a feat for Him to know whose hand had brushed His robe in an act of desperate faith. No, Jesus wasn't confused here. Nor did the bustling crowd or the humidity rolling off the Sea of Galilee muddle His mind. Our Savior chose to veil His omniscience for some reason. And I think the reason He veiled His knowledge of her identity was so He could heal her heart along with her body. I also think He wanted to teach the crowd a lesson about the significance of grace and the insignificance of reputation.

Do you need to touch the robe of Jesus? Is there a place in your heart that needs healing today?

The Whole Truth and Nothing but the Truth

Why do you think the woman came forward trembling? Well, remember the fact that she was considered unclean. She was probably scared to death that someone in the crowd would recognize her and yell indignantly, "Hey! It's the bloody lady! She's not supposed to be touching the Messiah!" She might have been afraid of Jesus' response too. What if He had said, "Woman, you're unclean. You have no right to touch the Son of God"? But He didn't. As a matter of fact, there must've been incredible compassion in His countenance because she went from cowering to chatting pretty quickly:

> Then the woman, knowing what had happened to her, came and fell at His feet and, trembling with fear, told Him the whole truth. (Mark 5:33)

Can you just imagine how long the *whole truth* was? She'd been sick for twelve years; doctors and friends had dismissed her; she'd been humiliated in bankruptcy court; she'd been the brunt of cruel jokes and even crueler gossip; and she'd been terribly lonely. She probably talked His ears off!

Jesus didn't have to listen to her whole truth. She was already healed. And besides, He needed to hustle because He had agreed to go to Jairus's house to heal the man's little girl, and they were running late. Jairus was a significant person, a community leader, a benefactor of the new Little League complex. His reputation as a business and spiritual leader was known all over the county. He was on everyone's bar mitzvah guestlist. This little woman, on the other hand, wasn't significant at all. The only reputation she had was as an unclean and unworthy person. She didn't have any money, and she hadn't been invited to any parties in more than a decade.

Still, the Lamb of God listened. He listened to her as she told Him the whole truth. He smiled indulgently when her timidity waned and her dramatic flair took over. He knew it had been a long time since she'd stood before anyone who cared enough to listen. And He knew that although her body was healed, her spirit was still sick. When she finally stopped to take a breath, He took her by the shoulders and called her the most beautiful name she'd ever been called: *daughter*. And in that moment, Jesus restored her peace, which had been pilfered for so many years.

I doubt she'd been dreaming about restoration when she woke up that morning. She had probably rolled over with a groan when the alarm went off, wondering how in the world she was going to make it through another twenty-four hours. She was tired of changing and washing her soiled bedclothes every day. Even more, she was tired of being considered unclean by everyone she knew. She was sick of being defined as the bleeding woman, the dirty woman, the woman who wasn't good enough to sit next to her neighbors in church. She was devastated that she was the only person in her little Galilean town who didn't have an orange-and-black headband hanging on her donkey.

But then, as mercy would have it, the God of all compassion walked into her world. And His grace radically rewrote her résumé. She went from being defined as a disreputable pariah to being called daughter:

> No longer will they call you Deserted, or name your land Desolate. But you will be called Hephzibah [which means "my delight is in her"] and your land

Beulah ["married"] for the LORD will take delight in you. (Isaiah 62:4)

Our wonderful, loving God wants to redeem us, not desert us. And He's sent His Son to define us—not by what we do, not by what others think of us, not even by what we think of ourselves, but by His own unfailing mercy and grace. May God grant us the wisdom to never rest in our reputations but only in the sure and living hope given to us through the grace of the gospel of Jesus Christ!

Hopeful Reflections

1. How important is your reputation to you?_____

    _____

    _____

    _____

    _____

    _____

    _____

    _____

    _____

    _____

2. Do you typically try to wash up before you approach the
    Savior, or do you run to Him when you're bleeding and
    unclean, figuratively speaking? _____

    _____

    _____

    _____

    _____

    _____

    _____

    _____

3. What do you usually have in your Tupperware when you
    approach God's banquet table? In other words, what
    "works of righteousness" do you tend to define yourself
    by?_____

    _____

_____

_____

_____

4. Have there been any "Leighs" in your life—people who really understood the grace of the gospel and taught you by their example? Consider writing them a letter to let them know about their influence on your spiritual journey. _____

_____

_____

_____

_____

_____

5. Read Psalm 139. Write down the memories you have from the first time you sensed the Lord calling you "daughter." When was the last time you sensed Him calling you His daughter?_____

_____

_____

_____

_____

_____

We have come to the wrong star....
That is what makes life at once so splendid
and so strange.
The true happiness is that we *don't* fit.
We come from somewhere else. We have lost our way.

—G. K. Chesterton

EIGHT

Homesick for Heaven

Sharks, Lizards, and Terrorized Tourists

Three summers ago I went on a ten-day "adventure" vacation to Belize, Central America, with my friend Julie. Both of us had dreamed of visiting the tropical paradise of Belize for years, and those dreams were finally coming true. We couldn't wait to hike the Mayan ruins and scuba-dive next to the second largest barrier reef in the world. We were also excited about diving in a place called "Shark and Ray Alley" where sharks and stingrays congregate in order to be fed by fishermen and tour guides.

I'd read about this site in a diving magazine and was intrigued and enticed. The article underscored the safety of the site; the sharks in Shark and Ray Alley are nurse sharks, which typically aren't dangerous. Their mouths are small, and their bite radius isn't big enough to sever an adult human appendage (i.e., an arm or a leg). That was good to know, since leaving Belize in one piece was high on our vacation wish list!

However, soon after our arrival we wondered if we'd

remain intact long enough to even go on the shark dive. The airport—which also functioned as a kind of Third World bazaar, bus shelter, and bar—was filled with pickpockets and scam artists. Julie and I were already nervous by the time our shuttle driver arrived. It didn't help that he decided to take a little detour through the inner city and leave us sitting and sweating in a back alley so he could "visit with his family." We weren't sure whether to applaud his devotion or prepare to be mugged! Then we had a bone-jarring, three-hour shuttle trip to our resort in the rain forest. When we finally collapsed in our hotel/hut, we were greeted by giant lizards staring down from the thatched roof above us. The lizards were quite friendly, we found out, because they grinned at us from the shower floor the next morning too. Our destination was definitely tropical, but to call it paradise would be pushing it!

We spent a few days hiking through ancient ruins and learning not to scream when really big reptiles ran toward us. We also got used to the taste of warm orange soda, which was the drink of choice since the local water made newcomers nauseous. Then we got ready for the next stop on our vacation itinerary. We piled our bags in a golf cart and puttered a few hundred yards to a red clay field where a charter plane was waiting to take us to the coast for the diving part of our trip. I know it

> OUR DESTINATION WAS DEFINITELY TROPICAL, BUT TO CALL IT PARADISE WOULD BE PUSHING IT!

sounds like a scene right out of an episode of *Fantasy Island*, but our "private plane" didn't look much safer than a paper version!

We barely squeezed our bodies and our luggage into the junior jet, and I literally held my breath when we barreled toward the trees at the end of the makeshift runway. I thought the pilot was going to ask us to heave out a bag or two so we could achieve liftoff. But somehow we squeaked over the treetops with a few feet to spare. I shouldn't complain, though; it's the only airplane I've ever flown in with the added feature of being able to enjoy the scenery below through holes in the floor!

Once we landed near the coast, we got settled into another thatched-roof, lizard-friendly room. We threw on some fresh native clothes and went in search of bottled water and a diving guide. We found some water sandwiched between cases of orange soda at a small grocery store on the island. Then we booked our shark dive with a jolly local man whose name—Goldie—was prominently tattooed across his generous tummy. He flashed us a gold-toothed grin and promised us an afternoon to remember, assuring us that he and his son had lots of experience swimming with and feeding the sharks and rays.

However, on the way to the dive site, Goldie warned us not to get our fingers near the sharks' mouths. They can't distinguish human hands from the squid they're fed, he explained, emphasizing this warning by gesturing toward his shy son's hands—which were missing a few fingers. Julie and I gave each other worried glances, wondering if we'd bitten off more than we could chew (no pun intended!).

As soon as the boat idled up to our destination, my apprehension was replaced by amazement. Right in front of us was a surreal scene of shark fins slicing through clear blue water dotted with the neon snorkels of other divers. I quickly flopped backward out of the boat with an underwater camera in my hand and my heart in my throat. The moment my mask cleared, I saw nurse sharks gliding by from every direction. They look like catfish on steroids—they have the same type of "whiskers" on their snouts! I couldn't believe I was swimming with real, live sharks, especially considering that I still get nervous watching *Jaws* reruns on cable. I was so dazed by their company, I forgot to breathe for a minute or so. I did remember to keep my hands balled into fists though!

> OUR LIVES MIGHT BE EXHILARATING AND/OR EXHAUSTING ADVENTURES—SOME PARTS GOOD, SOME PARTS BAD—BUT THIS WORLD STILL ISN'T OUR HOME.

Along with the sharks, stingrays swam above and beneath me like huge, graceful birds. And tropical fish of every imaginable shape and color were everywhere. I twisted, turned, rolled, and swiveled, trying to take in every scene of this incredible underwater ballet. I've never seen anything quite like it.

Our entire Central American sabbatical, in fact, left me feeling acutely aware that I was in an unfamiliar world. This is a place where you can swim with sharks, go to restaurants barefoot, and watch toucans fly overhead with their laughably large beaks. A place where you fly at your own risk, where air-conditioning is rarer than a four-leafed clover (except on perforated planes!), and where clean drinking water is a luxury. I felt like crying out with Dorothy in the *Wizard of Oz*, "Toto, we're not in Kansas anymore!" Belize was an exhilarating and exhausting adventure—some parts good, some parts bad—but it wasn't home. Julie and I were definitely strangers in a strange land.

Have you ever felt like that—a foreigner in a strange land?
Even in the middle of your familiar life?

The truth is, as Christians we live in a place where we really don't belong. The Bible says we are all aliens and strangers here (1 Peter 2:11), and Jesus Himself said:

> If you belonged to the world, it would love you as its own. As it is, you do not belong to the world, but I have chosen you out of the world. That is why the world hates you. (John 15:19)

Pretty strong words from our Savior establishing us, His disciples, as resident aliens. We live here, pay taxes here, eat too much cholesterol here, and we might just get buried here. But as God's immortal children, our present realities don't accurately define us. Our lives might be exhilarating and/or exhausting adventures—some parts good, some parts bad—but this world still isn't our home. That encourages me even more than finding out that nurse sharks have mini-mouths. Because if this world were it—if present reality was the best I could hope for—I think I'd be pretty darn depressed. Facing lizards in the living room is no big deal compared to facing some of life's heartbreaks and disappointments!

When Wishes Don't Come True

I turned thirty-six this year, and it was a good birthday, as birthdays go. My coworkers arranged a party where I got lots of hugs, opened presents, and ate dark chocolate cake. Then I went to a gourmet dinner with my sweet friend, Kim, and ate more delicious, fattening things. (Calories don't count on your birthday, right?) But after I got home that night and treated my indigestion, I realized I wasn't really satisfied. As the memories of the day washed over me, I felt strangely sad, as if I had an upset soul.

I really was thankful for everyone's thoughtfulness—for all the laughter and funny cards at work and for a dear friend who went out of her way to make me feel special. But I wanted something else. I wanted to have dinner with my very own family. I wanted to open a silly present I might not even like from a husband I really loved. I wanted to hear little voices sing, "Happy birthday to you, happy birthday to you. Happy birthday dear Mommy, happy birthday to you." I cried myself to sleep that night.

You've probably been there before. Maybe you haven't wished for a husband and children for your birthday; maybe you just wished for a *different* husband and *quieter* children! But I'll bet you can identify with the disappointment that comes with not getting what you've hoped for. Maybe

SOMETIMES WE FEEL SO OUT OF PLACE IN THIS WORLD. WE BECOME HOME-SICK FOR HEAVEN.

you hoped and prayed for a different diagnosis. Or maybe you hoped for a bigger balance in the bank when the bills rolled in. Maybe you've simply hoped that someone would love you well. And maybe you've cried alone at night too.

I'm sure you're familiar with the Bible verse that says God will give us the desires of our heart (Psalm 37:4). But even though we know His Word is true, sometimes we still long for things to be different, to be better. We get weary of wanting and waiting. We wish God would heal our hurts faster. Sometimes we feel so out of place in this world. We become homesick for heaven.

When was the last time you thought about heaven?

Jesus told a short story in Matthew about five women who longed for glory. I think He told this tale to remind us to keep hoping for heaven even though we have to live in present-day reality:

> At that time the kingdom of heaven will be like ten virgins who took their lamps and went out to meet the bridegroom. Five of them were foolish and five

Chapter 8: *Homesick for Heaven* 117

were wise. The foolish ones took their lamps but did not take any oil with them. The wise, however, took oil in jars along with their lamps. The bridegroom was a long time in coming, and they all became drowsy and fell asleep.

At midnight the cry rang out: "Here's the bridegroom! Come out to meet him!"

Then all the virgins woke up and trimmed their lamps. The foolish ones said to the wise, "Give us some of your oil; our lamps are going out."

"No," they replied, "there may not be enough for both us and you. Instead, go to those who sell oil and buy some for yourselves."

But while they were on their way to buy the oil, the bridegroom arrived. The virgins who were ready went in with him to the wedding banquet. And the door was shut.

Later the others also came. "Sir! Sir!" they said. "Open the door for us!"

But he replied, "I tell you the truth, I don't know you."

Therefore keep watch, because you do not know the day or the hour. (Matthew 25:1–13)

Contrary to first impressions, Jesus wasn't encouraging His listeners to be petroleum piglets! Many theological scholars believe the oil in the story symbolizes faith in God or spiritual preparedness.[1] So lesson number one is that salvation isn't transferable; we can't borrow someone else's. For example, just because your parents are believers and you grew up in a Christian home doesn't mean you are a Christian, any more than sitting in McDonald's makes you a cheeseburger. We have to come to our own individual repentance and faith in Christ. Jesus went on to emphasize the importance of being ready for His return. So lesson number two is that being saved doesn't justify being a spiritual couch potato. We don't have a license to lounge in La-Z-Boys until we fly away to glory.

⌒

BEING SAVED DOESN'T JUSTIFY BEING A SPIRITUAL COUCH POTATO. WE DON'T HAVE A LICENSE TO LOUNGE IN LA-Z-BOYS UNTIL WE FLY AWAY TO GLORY.

In order to better understand these points and get the main message, we need a little tutoring in Jewish wedding tradition. During the time of Christ, when a Jewish couple got engaged, the actual marriage ceremony didn't take place for a year or two. Still the man and woman were considered husband and wife (just not allowed to engage in sexual relations), and the arrangement couldn't be "undone" without a formal divorce. Remember how Joseph had in mind to divorce Mary, even though they hadn't slept together yet? How unlike our culture, where as long as the couple-to-be returns the expensive gifts, they can break off the engagement at any time—right up to the "I do."

The Jewish groom-to-be usually spent the time between the engagement and the wedding feast preparing a place for the couple to live. Sometimes he'd build a room over his parents' house (an "upper room"). If he'd been really discerning with his denarii, he might even be able to afford their own house. I guess he kept the lid on his libido by lifting heavy building materials!

While the groom was off arranging their abode, the bride-to-be planned for his imminent return. Her season of betrothal was full of preparations for their wedding feast. Exuberant relatives would be coming in from all over Israel for the weeklong celebration, so she stayed pretty busy meeting with caterers and party planners. She also spent a lot of time making herself more beautiful for her beloved. (I'm not sure what they called personal trainers back then, but most brides probably had one!)

If her groom lived in another village, she might not communicate with him at all between their engagement and the wedding ceremony, making the exact day and time of his return a mystery. So she kept one eye on the door while she worked, anxiously waiting for someone to burst through and tell her the groom was on his way. She probably tossed and turned at night, wondering when he would finally come back for her. The room she shared with her sisters probably felt to her like a little girl's room that she'd outgrown. As much as she loved her family, she just didn't belong there anymore. She was promised in marriage, and she couldn't wait to move into a new home with her husband.[2]

WHEN WE PUT OUR FAITH IN CHRIST, WE BECOME OFFICIALLY ENGAGED TO THE SON OF GOD.

I think Jesus purposely chose the Jewish tradition of courtship as the context for His lesson because He wants us to live as if we're in the year of our betrothal. When we put our faith in Christ, we become officially engaged to the Son of God. We are His bride, promised in marriage, but not yet living with Him. We need to be preparing for our wedding feast. There are people to invite and parties to plan! We should be conscientiously making ourselves more beautiful for our beloved Bridegroom. This world isn't our real home anymore; and just as the starry-eyed Jewish bride waited expectantly for her groom's return, so should we.

Hope for the Hopeless

My friend Jim was called to the hospital in Denver a few years ago to visit a man named Don. Don's daughter had accidentally backed the family car over him when he was working on it, leaving him permanently paralyzed from the neck down. Jim said he was taken aback when he walked into the hospital room and saw Don's appearance. A stainless steel band, which was fastened to his skull with long screws, surrounded his shaved head. Tubes and wires monitoring every beat and tick sprouted from his arms like pipe cleaners.

Jim made small talk with Don but later admitted he was very uncomfortable. What in the world could he say to encourage a man who would never again move anything other than the muscles in his face? I can picture big, sweet Jim fidgeting in a plastic chair during the awkward gaps in their conversation. After a while Jim got up and stood in front of the bed so Don could see his face. The only thing he could think of to do was pray. So he asked Don if he could pray for him before he left. Don said he'd like that, but he had something he wanted to say first.

Don looked directly into Jim's eyes and said, "I know in the depths of my soul that God's sovereignty will never take me to a place where His grace can't sustain me." He told Jim that even though he would never walk again, he knew God loved him. He believed God was faithful regardless of his circumstances. His confident voice rose above the hum of the machines sustaining his broken body as he talked about God's goodness.

My two-hundred-and-fifty-pound, mountain-of-a-man, tender-hearted friend cried all the way back to Colorado Springs. Jim was deeply moved by Don's faith and reminded of how God's love elevates us from the bruising boundaries of this world.

How about you? Does the reality of God's love for you lift you above your present problems?

Realistically, I'm sure Don has days when he doesn't feel so peaceful. There are probably lots of times when he watches other fathers from his wheelchair and wishes he could walk beside his daughters or carry the littlest one on his shoulders. But then he remembers this world isn't his home. He remembers that his spirit isn't confined to a chair. We need to remember that too—that whatever our reality, it can't begin to define those of us who are loved by the Lamb of God.

Paul must have been remembering this when he wrote:

> I have learned to be content whatever the circumstances. I know what it is to be in need, and I know what it is to have plenty. I have learned the secret of being content in any and every situation, whether well fed or hungry, whether living in plenty or in want. I can do everything through him who gives me strength. (Philippians 4:11–13)

With God's help we can learn to be content regardless of our circumstances—even *in spite* of our circumstances. Remember, this world is not our home. Let us fix our eyes on Jesus as we prepare for our wedding feast. Because one day our Bridegroom will come for us and take us to the place He's prepared especially for you and me.

WHATEVER OUR REALITY, IT CAN'T BEGIN TO DEFINE THOSE OF US WHO ARE LOVED BY THE LAMB OF GOD.

Hopeful Reflections

1. Have you ever felt like a stranger in a foreign land? Why?_____

   _____

   _____

   _____

   _____

   _____

   _____

   _____

2. When was the last time you cried alone because you were disappointed about something? _____

   _____

   _____

   _____

   _____

3. How often do you think about heaven? Sometime this week spend at least ten minutes outside lying on your back, looking up at the clouds, and pondering heaven. If the ground is covered in snow, make a "snow angel" while you're at it! _____

   _____

   _____

   _____

_____

_____

4. Rent the movie *Shadowlands* (it's about the life of C. S. Lewis) and watch it with a close friend or your husband. Spend some time afterward discussing how it made you feel and why._____

    _____

    _____

    _____

    _____

    _____

5. Read Habakkuk 3:17–18. Meditate on this passage (it might help to print it on an index card and put it in a place where you will see it often). Pray that God would give you His perspective regarding your circumstances.

    _____

    _____

    _____

    _____

    _____

    _____

Part 3: *beloved by God*

Strangely enough, the lens of grace reveals those outside the church in the very same light. Like me, like everyone inside the church, they too are sinners loved by God.

—Philip Yancey

NINE

Witnesses to His Grace

Leaning against a Lamb

So far we've talked about the criteria for being women of hope. We've acknowledged our desperate need for God's mercy, recognizing we can't save ourselves. And we've started rewriting our résumés in order to be defined by His grace instead of our riches, relationships, reputations, or present realities. Basically we've pondered the parameters for *who we are* as His daughters. Now let's consider *how we should live* as women beloved by God.

Michie (pronounced "Micky") and Michele Hill, my friend Kim's parents, run their house like an effective, non-profit Humane Society. But they don't specialize in cat and dog adoption or neutering programs; they specialize in people. They take in strays of all kinds, usually young men and women who've been banged up in the rough game of life. They don't take a salary, and their generosity doesn't make headlines. Michie and Michele give their "strays" free room and board and lots of compassion. They also help them get jobs, get plugged into Bible studies, and get involved in relationships with other Christians their age. (And unlike the Humane Society that takes in unwanted pets, the Hills' guests are never euthanized!)

Kim says her mom and dad have taken in brokenhearted boarders for as long as she can remember. It wasn't at all unusual for her to come home from school and find out someone had moved into her room for a week or two (or three, or four…). She didn't always appreciate her parents' mission, especially when she had to give up her room to a stranger and bunk with her little sister! But when she got older, she began to realize what a rare treasure their generosity was. And one day she actually volunteered to give up her room for someone else. Of course, she wasn't living at home anymore!

Kim had just recently moved to Nashville to pursue a career in music when she met a young man named Jose at a summer camp where she was a counselor. Jose was a new Christian, earnestly trying to honor God with his life but struggling with all kinds of problems. After hearing his story, Kim immediately thought her parents could help get him on the right track. She called her mom and explained the situation.

"Of course he can stay here," Michele said. "Tell him to head to Memphis, and I'll get his room ready."

Several hours later there was a knock on the door at the Hill house, and Michele opened it to find a young, clean-cut Hispanic man standing on the doorstep. She quickly leaned forward and embraced him, saying, "Welcome! We're so glad you're finally here! Please come in and make yourself at home. Our house is your house." But the young man just stood there rigidly. Michele thought, *Poor little guy. He doesn't even know how to respond to kindness.* So she leaned forward again and hugged him harder, repeating her greeting with even more enthusiasm. He remained stiff and unresponsive and appeared nervous. As she released him from the second unrequited embrace, she noticed a large metal canister by his side. Then she noticed a white truck with a familiar logo in the driveway. Suddenly she realized she had been affectionately accosting the pest control man!

Michele is a great example of God's love; if you get within an arm's reach, you're going to get hugged, patted, or invited to dinner. She's kind of like the log flume ride at the amusement park—grace sloshes out, and even the bystanders in her life get wet! She firmly believes that loving people well is her job description as a Christian. I think that's exactly what Jesus was talking about when He said:

> By this all men will know that you are my disciples, if you love one another. (John 13:35)

Michie and Michele look like His disciples. Their lives are a witness to His amazing grace.

⌒What about you? Have you ever been accused of "sloshing grace" on the people who get close to you?

The Big Squeeze

The apostle John emphasizes being a witness for the love of Christ throughout his Gospel account. He shows the Messiah massaging His disciples' callused and dusty feet and recounts His compassionate command urging them to follow His example and wash each other's feet (John 13:1–14). It was John who recorded Jesus' moving monologue in which He called the disciples His "friends" and once again commanded them to love each other just as He had loved them (John 15:12–15). He is also the only New Testament writer who refers to Jesus as the *Lamb* of God (John 1:29; 1:36; and thirty times in Revelation). This tender title illustrates Jesus' love for us—a love that led Him to offer Himself like "a lamb to the slaughter" (Isaiah 53:7). John's entire Gospel is riddled with the language of love. He even refers to himself as "the one Jesus loved" not once or twice, but five times!

I used to think that referring to yourself as "the one Jesus loved" was a bit much, kind of like love-bragging! It seemed awfully presumptuous, even arrogant. Was John trying to be the Teacher's pet? I could picture the other disciples listening to him claiming Christ's affection and exchanging sideways glances that echoed loudly their "Oh brother, here he goes again!" sentiments.

But then I studied one little verse that appears at the end of John's Gospel account—one short sentence holding the secret to John's secure self-image and the key to having a life riddled with the language of love:

> Peter turned and saw that the disciple whom Jesus loved was following them. (This was the one who had leaned back against Jesus at the supper and had said, "Lord, who is going to betray you?") (John 21:20)

I know, I know, it doesn't seem like a very significant verse. It's just one tiny part of the scene John is narrating about a conversation between Jesus and Peter. But let's look a little closer at the sentence in parentheses:

(This was the one who had leaned back against Jesus at the supper and had said, "Lord, who is going to betray you?")

That sentence has become one of my favorite sentences in the Bible. I think it explains John's preoccupation with love. John wrote that parenthetical remark at the end of his life, probably about fifty years after the Last Supper had taken place. Much had happened since that symbolic supper. He may have smiled when he wrote this, remembering what a naive teenager he'd been then. He wasn't naive anymore. He'd been awestruck when a tornado-like wind that blew through a Pentecost party he was attending turned out to be the Holy Spirit. He'd watched a crippled man, healed through the power of Jesus' name, turn cartwheels in front of the horrified faces of the same men who plotted to kill Jesus. He'd also been jailed, beaten, and lived like a homeless refugee for the sake of the gospel.[1]

Yes, a lot had happened in the previous fifty years—but nothing as significant as the embrace he had shared with the Prince of Peace. He'd been held by the God who holds the moon and the stars in His mighty hand. The Lamb of God let him recline and feel the rise and fall of His breast. The memory of leaning against Jesus lingered in John's heart and mind for the rest of his life. It seared his soul with a sense of belonging and being loved. Nothing else compared. There weren't any letters after his name distinguishing him as a scholar or a doctor, just a short parenthetical remark defining John as being loved by Jesus. Leaning on Jesus symbolized the intimacy of their relationship, and it was the way John chose to describe himself. "I'm the one who got to lean against Jesus!" John was a witness to the Lamb's love because he had experienced the Lamb's love.

Have you experienced the love of God? If so, is your life a witness to that amazing grace?

Chocolate-Covered Compassion

One of my mom's favorite stories about me as a little girl climaxes with a jumbo-size box of Junior Mints. If you don't know what Junior Mints are, they're like tiny Peppermint Patties—dark chocolate outside and peppermint creme inside. They're still sold at some stores, and you can almost always buy them at the movies. (If you happen to feel the urge to get some, please know that they melt into a big, gooey mess if you leave them in a hot car. Trust me on that one.)

Anyway, the story happened at Christmastime when I was in the second grade. The day to exchange Christmas presents with classmates had finally arrived, and my friends and I were very excited. (This was in the good old days, long before "Merry Christmas" was replaced with "Happy Holidays," courtesy of the ACLU.) We'd been planning our class Christmas party for weeks, and the highlight of our celebration was the gift exchange. We'd been firmly instructed to spend no more than fifty cents on a gift. (Again, this was in the good old days, when fifty cents meant your Tooth Fairy was rich!) I remember daydreaming about what special treasure—a yo-yo or an Astro-Pop?—I should buy with my two quarters to put under the class Christmas tree.

The morning of the party we all pranced up the steps of Southside Elementary School, clutching our brightly wrapped packages. Much of our excitement was braided to the mystery of the exchange. None of us knew who was going to receive the gift we'd painstakingly picked out. And none of

> THE MEMORY OF LEANING AGAINST JESUS LINGERED IN JOHN'S HEART AND MIND FOR THE REST OF HIS LIFE. IT SEARED HIS SOUL WITH A SENSE OF BELONGING AND BEING LOVED.

us knew whose gift we were going to open. Our teacher had figured out some type of numbering system that governed the whole Christmas present process, but to this day I'm not sure how she did it. I think it involved logarithms!

Nonetheless, after cookies and punch we were directed to our desks to await the disclosure of who would open which gift. We squirmed in our seats, wondering which box from the gleaming pile of presents under the tree would be ours. Then the classroom door creaked and in walked Mary Williams, holding a clumsily wrapped box. Mary was quiet and shy and came from a very poor inner-city family. Several of the kids groaned as she shuffled to her seat and whispered things like, "I sure hope I don't have to open *that* gift!"

There was a moment of awkward silence while our teacher no doubt tried to figure out how to make the gift exchange work with the addition of Mary and her pitiful present. Suddenly I piped up and said, "May I please exchange presents with Mary, Mrs. Carlton?" I don't remember exactly how everything transpired, but I got to exchange presents with Mary. I also don't remember what I gave her. But I vividly remember the giant box of candy she gave me. It was a colossal crate of Junior Mints, bigger than anything they had at the movie theater! It was obvious the box had

> I SURE HOPE I'D STILL GLADLY OFFER TO EXCHANGE GIFTS WITH AN INSECURE WOMAN HOLDING A BOX WRAPPED IN NEWSPAPER.

cost much more than fifty cents. All the other kids crowded around my desk with "oohs" and "aahs" and enthusiastic offers to trade presents. That big box of chocolate mints stood out like a strand of pearls next to plastic beads. Mary smiled a lot that day.

When I got home from school, I told my mom all about our Christmas party. She had probably already guessed what kind of present I'd opened because I'm sure there were telltale signs of chocolate smeared across my mouth! After dinner Mrs. Carlton called and told Mom about my mercy at the gift exchange. She raved about my kindness, saying what a special child I was. She said the whole thing reminded her of the miracle of Christmas. Mom was proud.

I want to be kind and tender-hearted today like I was back then. I sure hope I'd still gladly offer to exchange gifts with an insecure woman holding a box wrapped in newspaper. But my actions aren't the point of this story. That gift-exchange kindness wasn't as much about what I'd given as it was about what I'd received. When I carried my nicely wrapped package to school that morning, I also carried the assurance of my mother's love. I knew, as much as a seven-year-old can know anything, that my mom loved me. I knew that if I went home that afternoon and asked her to come out back and sit on the swing and talk, she would. And I knew that I could lean against her while we rocked back and forth. It was natural for me to be kind to Mary because I was a little girl who had experienced great kindness and love.

Dancing in the Rain

John and his brother James are referred to in the Gospel of Mark as the "Sons of Thunder." Theologians aren't sure why they were called that, but it probably had something to do with the strength of their personalities. Their stormy moniker certainly doesn't conjure up images of gentle and kind men musing about washing other people's feet and laying down their lives for their friends!

But the gift of love that Jesus gave John changed his personality. His thunder quieted down when he leaned against the Savior and listened to the steady beat of His heart. John began to call his followers "dear friends" and "children" in his letters and said that he'd much rather visit and talk with them face to face than use paper and ink (2 John 12). Instead of running for cover when they heard John's thunder, people began to dance in the rain of his mercy. John looked like a disciple of Jesus because of the way he loved people. And John loved people because he knew he was the one whom Jesus loved. He lived his life as a wonderful witness to the grace of the gospel.

JOHN LOOKED LIKE A DISCIPLE OF JESUS BECAUSE OF THE WAY HE LOVED PEOPLE. AND JOHN LOVED PEOPLE BECAUSE HE KNEW HE WAS THE ONE WHOM JESUS LOVED.

Do you look like a disciple of Jesus? Do people run to the love of God they see in you, or do they run for cover?

The truth is you and I are also the ones whom Jesus loves. He laid down His life to show us the full extent of His great love for us. May we be witnesses to that mercy, love, and grace to the people around us.

Hopeful Reflections

1. When was the last time, figuratively speaking, that you leaned against Jesus and listened to His heartbeat?

   _____

   _____

   _____

   _____

   _____

   _____

2. Do you witness about His kindness and mercy because you know that you're one whom Jesus loves? _____

   _____

   _____

   _____

   _____

   _____

   _____

3. Make a list of people you care about who don't know Jesus. Read 1 Peter 3:15 and pray that God would give you an opportunity to "give an answer...for the hope that you have" to each of the lost lambs on your list.

   _____

   _____

   _____

_____

_____

_____

4. Consider taking or reviewing a class in relationship-based evangelism (for example, *Contagious Christianity*, produced by Willow Creek Community Church in Chicago). If no classes are available, read a book on this subject. _____

_____

_____

_____

_____

_____

_____

_____

_____

Our thoughts of God
are all too human.

—Martin Luther

TEN

Walking in Godly Wisdom

Movies, Marathons, and BLTs

One of the first things on my mother's "to-do" list when she gets to heaven is to find Kathleen Jumper. Kathleen was Mom's spiritual mentor, counselor, teacher, and dearest friend. She walked Mom through some of the darkest periods in her life. The few times I got to visit Kathleen I felt like I was in the presence of greatness. She was kind and humble but carried herself with such dignity and grace that she seemed almost regal. I asked her lots of questions about the Lord, and she gave me thoughtful answers, often quoting directly from Scripture. It seemed she had most of the Bible memorized.

Eleven years ago Kathleen was counseling someone on the phone when she exclaimed, "Hallelujah!" then fell to the floor dead from a massive heart attack. Mom says it was just like Kathleen to be helping someone right up until the minute she walked into the arms of God. She was always giving to others—feeding the hungry, praying for the brokenhearted, housing the homeless. She lived God's command to "consider others better than yourselves" (Philippians 2:3).

Kathleen was a simple retired high school music teacher. She didn't have any seminary diplomas on the walls of her little house nestled in the Smoky Mountains. But Kathleen Jumper was shrouded in wisdom. Mom insists Kathleen was the wisest woman she's ever known, and although I didn't know her that well, I'm inclined to agree. I also think Kathleen's selflessness was the sweetest fruit of her wisdom. Her long walk with Christ led her to the knowledge that life wasn't all about *her*.

Egocentric Cinema

Last week I heard a twenty-year-old give her testimony to a group of high school girls. I got tickled listening to her talk because she was so emotive. The highs and lows of her life were recited with the flair of an Academy Award–winning actress. A recent breakup with her boyfriend was recounted with all the melodrama of Juliet's farewell to Romeo. Listening to her tell her life story was like watching a movie in an IMAX theater—you know, one of those new theaters with surround-sound systems and huge screens that show three-dimensional, larger-than-life images.

Later that night I was smiling to myself and thinking about how narcissistic most college coeds are when I realized that watching her was like looking in a mirror. Maturity has tempered my melodrama a little bit, so I don't talk about myself quite as loudly or colorfully as this college girl did. But I'm still a card-carrying member of the egocentric cinema. I'm a walking, talking, me-MAX theater, proudly screening a movie with yours truly in the starring role! My movie can be so mesmerizing that I get distracted into thinking that life's all about Lisa Harper. Unlike Kathleen, I often assume my world revolves around me. And sometimes I'd like for everyone else's world to revolve around me too!

> I OFTEN ASSUME MY WORLD REVOLVES AROUND ME. AND SOMETIMES I'D LIKE FOR EVERYONE ELSE'S WORLD TO REVOLVE AROUND ME TOO!

But the funny thing about me-MAX movies is that everyone else is so involved in their own productions that they can't pay much attention to ours. Haven't you shared some gripping drama in your life with a friend at one time or another, only to have her respond with something like, "Hmm, that's interesting. Now let me tell you more about me"?

Egocentric cinema is a self-centered show. Some people try to spice up their movies in order to make them more interesting, hoping high drama will lure an audience. They weep long and loud in public and graphically describe their trials and tribulations until someone takes notice. (You've probably had a "dramatic disciple" in one of your Bible studies or small groups. She's usually the whiny one who commandeers the conversation and talks about herself the whole time!) But in the end their movies are still just one of millions, and the audience goes home, drawn back to their own flickering screens.

A. W. Tozer commented on our self-involvement in his book *The Pursuit of God*: "Within the human heart things have taken over. Men have now by nature no peace within their hearts, for God is crowned there no longer, but there in the moral dusk, stubborn and aggressive usurpers fight among themselves for the first place on the throne."[1]

Recently I had lunch with the president of a Christian publishing company. Since I've coauthored a few books, it wasn't the first time I'd met with a publisher. But it was still a significant event. This time I was meeting with a man who had offered me a contract to write a book *all by myself*. I kept hoping that one of my friends would call the office that morning so I could say, "I'm sorry, but I can't chat for long. I've got a meeting with my publisher." Of course the phone never rang, so I couldn't impress anyone with my newfound "actual author" status. Still I felt proud as I drove to the restaurant. It's not every day that I get to meet with a head honcho in the publishing world!

We had a great visit over lunch. Then as we were leaving he said, "Kim, I'd like to get your home address for my Rolodex." I thought, *Did he just call me "Kim"? Maybe he just pronounced "Lisa" weird.* But I could read the upside-down writing in his notebook next to the address line, and it said "K–I–M" in big, black letters. Here I was, thinking I was on the cusp of literary greatness, and my publisher didn't even know my name. Obviously I'm not nearly as important as I think I am!

I believe self-centered cinema is one of the most aggressive usurpers of godly wisdom. Loving God and others has taken a backseat to the consuming daily drama of our lives. Self-infatuation has deluded us into thinking that we're much more important than we really are. As His daughters, we have been called to close our me-MAX theaters. One of the wisest things we can do is to acknowledge and practice the simple biblical truth that life isn't all about us. We need to have the same attitude as Jesus:

> For even the Son of Man did not come to be served, but to serve, and to give his life as a ransom for many. (Mark 10:45)

Frightening Food Groups

Not only is life not all about us, it's not all up to us either. I was reminded of this a few years ago when my friend Judy talked me into entering a road race in Denver, Colorado. I didn't really want to run in the race. I was a college athlete and have competed in many other sports, but long-distance running has never been one of my favorites. I must have the runner's equivalent of attention deficit disorder; any distance over three miles is about as enjoyable as chewing sand to me. Judy, on the other hand, is a natural distance runner with very long legs and very little body fat.

LOVING GOD AND OTHERS HAS TAKEN A BACKSEAT TO THE CONSUMING DAILY DRAMA OF OUR LIVES.

She finished in the top five at the Pike's Peak Marathon (which boasts a field of world-class runners), in which competitors have to run thirteen and a half miles up Pike's Peak and then turn around and career back down the rocky mountain trail.

Judy and her long-legged, lungs-of-steel buddies were way out of my league! Still she persisted, saying it would be fun for me to run the race with her (make that way behind her), and I could think of it as a great workout. Plus, she added, I'd get a cute T-shirt. (She knows I've always been a sucker for cute T-shirts.) So before sunrise on the morning of the race, when my alarm clock went off in Colorado Springs, I groggily rolled out of bed with a feeling of foreboding. Feelings of foreboding at five in the morning should not be ignored.

Judy looked chipper while we were driving to Denver— as if she was actually looking forward to what lay ahead. My face, on the other hand, was drawn with a thousand worries. What if I come in dead last? What if I get violently sick during the race and scare innocent children? What if the course officials pull me out of the race because they have to reopen the roads to downtown traffic? By the time we got to the race site, my stomach was in knots. And to make matters worse, snow was falling, and I hadn't thought to bring tights or a sweatshirt. *If I could just eat a warm donut and drink some hot chocolate, I'll be fine*, I thought. But I didn't want to be the only person with a number pinned to my shirt wolfing down snacks. So I just shivered and grimaced and waited alongside lots of thin, perky people for the race to begin.

As soon as the starter's pistol sounded, we were off like horses headed for the barn. For a mile or so I was right up there with the front runners, racing along at a steady clip. I thought maybe a genetic miracle had taken place in my sleep and I had evolved into an overnight running sensation. But what had actually happened was that my pride had been pricked by the cheering fans lining the downtown section of the racecourse. I've always performed well in front of a crowd—some people refer to it as "Kodak courage"—and as long as people were cheering, I ran like a fleet-footed gazelle.

I'VE ALWAYS PERFORMED WELL IN FRONT OF A CROWD—SOME PEOPLE REFER TO IT AS "KODAK COURAGE"—AND AS LONG AS PEOPLE WERE CHEERING, I RAN LIKE A FLEET-FOOTED GAZELLE.

Soon enough, however, the course turned away from downtown Denver and started winding up a steep hill. The roar of the fans faded into the distance until all I could hear was my own ragged breathing. It was wet and cold and miserable. The race wasn't even half over, and I was looking for potholes to step in so I could "accidentally" twist my ankle and hobble off the course with some stolen dignity. I was daydreaming of donuts and thinking to myself that quitting would be more honorable than faking an injury when I noticed a commotion to my right. I looked over my shoulder and was surprised to see a giant bacon-lettuce-and-tomato sandwich jogging next to me. The meal on wheels was made up of three teenage boys, tied together and wearing huge foam cutouts spray-painted to look just like a BLT. The first boy was dressed like a seven-foot-tall piece of Wonder Bread, trailing a very lifelike leaf of lettuce. The second young man trotted quickly behind him with only his face poking through enormous strips of plastic bacon, glued to a tomato wedge of horror-movie proportions. Merrily bringing up the rear was another grinning slice of Wonder Bread, slathered in painted-on mustard. They were wearing the biggest, most creative costume I've ever seen at a sporting event. And they were passing me.

I couldn't believe it! I've played college volleyball, raced mountain bikes, and hiked fourteen-thousand-foot mountains; yet here I was, getting beat by a sandwich! Something stirred deep within my old athletic soul. I just couldn't let a food group beat me to the finish line! What would Judy think? What would I tell my grandchildren? My vision narrowed, and my mind was overtaken by the desperate, primitive urge to win. I blocked out the cold, the cramps, and the chocolate croissant cravings and picked up the pace. If this bounding BLT was going to be defeated, it was up to me.

Pretty soon it became apparent that we were running a race within a race. Neither one of us was going to overtake

> I GET SO FOCUSED ON THE MINUTIAE OF MY BATTLES THAT I FORGET GOD HAS ALREADY WON THE WAR.

the leaders; we were in about 109th and 110th place, respectively. But we were running as if our lives depended on beating each other. We were neck and neck as we crested the last hill and began the descent toward the finish line. Hundreds of people were anxiously watching our dramatic duel from the bottom of the hill, and most of them were rooting for the more photograph-friendly lunch-on-legs. At the last possible moment, wincing in pain, I pressed into the lead and crossed the finish line just ahead of the BLT boys. I think their collective wind resistance gave me a slight edge.

What sandwiches have been nipping at your heels lately? Are you overwhelmed by a rebellious teenager? Desperately trying to win back a husband who doesn't seem to love you anymore? Hoping to outrun a past that keeps overtaking your heart and mind? Do you think overcoming these obstacles is all up to you?

Sometimes I do. Just as my vision narrowed to the single goal of outrunning the sandwich, my mind-set often narrows to the self-centered purpose of defeating the difficulties in my life. I block out everything else and pick up the pace because I think I've got to beat my problems on my own. The discordant melody of "grit your teeth and try harder…gut it out…no pain, no gain" plays over and over in my head. Finally I get so focused on the minutiae of my battles that I forget God has already won the war. My masochistic mind-set—thinking that it's all up to me—causes me to miss God's mercy.

Chapter 10: *Walking in Godly Wisdom*   151

As Christian women, most of us would say we believe in the doctrine of God's sovereignty. We nod our heads in agreement that He is omnipotent and omniscient, that He is above all and over all. We verbally acknowledge that God is in control. But we can't shake the fact that we're women. By hormonal default we think we should be in control because—if the truth were told—everything is up to us. Right? If we don't do the laundry, the whole country will be dressed in foul-smelling rags. If we don't cook, our families will starve or die from salmonella poisoning. If we don't go shopping, the entire global economy will grind to a halt.

How often have you said something like, "If I don't do it, it won't get done"? Or, "If I don't do it, it won't be done right"? Have you been blinded by your battles? Are you so myopic that you're missing out on God's mercy?

My mother told me that when she was preoccupied with the biggest battle of her life, she went to Kathleen Jumper for counsel, believing her friend would offer great wisdom. Mom sobbed as she shared the fears and problems resulting from my little brother's drug addiction. She was really disappointed when Kathleen sent her home with the advice to stop despairing and read the story of Asa in 2 Chronicles.

Mom drove away frustrated but dutifully opened her Bible to the Old Testament when she got home and read about Asa, the king of Judah and father of Jehoshaphat. She said that as she read the passage recounting Asa's reign, she couldn't understand why Kathleen had wanted her to read it.

It didn't seem to have anything whatsoever to do with the battle she was fighting. Confused, she reread the story to see if maybe she'd overlooked something. And finally, on the third reading, Mom found the treasure she'd been digging for.

In the thirty-sixth year of his reign, Asa got over-whelmed in a race with a sandwich named Baasha. He tried to defeat his opponent on his own by making a treaty with another king instead on trusting in God's protection. Afterward a seer named Hanani—kind of a plucky Christian counselor—came to Asa and confronted him:

> Because you relied on the king of Aram and not on the LORD your God, the army of the king of Aram has escaped from your hand. Were not the Cushites and Libyans a mighty army with great numbers of chariots and horsemen? Yet when you relied on the LORD, He delivered them into your hand. For the eyes of the LORD range throughout the earth to strengthen those whose hearts are fully committed to him. You have done a foolish thing, and from now on you will be at war. (2 Chronicles 16:7–9)

In other words, Asa acquiesced to the fear that *it was all up to him* instead of standing firm in his faith. He was so blinded by the battle with Baasha that he forgot God's sovereign faithfulness. Mom recognized herself in old king Asa. She said she realized that she could either put her trust in God or trust in her own strength. She had a choice to go on desperately trying to fix John and single-handedly defeat the drug addiction that held him captive, or she could put her hope and trust in God's faithfulness and rest in the belief that her son's salvation was not all up to her. Mom decided she wasn't big enough to win this race by herself.

Each of us has formidable foes. Sometimes there are some pretty scary-looking sandwiches bearing down on us. But we do not have to run the race by ourselves. We are the precious daughters of the Creator of the universe, and He is unbeatable. Listen to His promise to us:

> Fear not, for I have redeemed you; I have summoned you by name; you are mine. When you pass through the waters, I will be with you; and when you pass through the rivers, they will not sweep over you. When you walk through the fire, you will not be burned; the flames will not set you ablaze. For I am the LORD, your God, the Holy One of Israel, your Savior; I give Egypt for your ransom, Cush and Seba in your stead. Since you are precious and honored in my sight, and because I love you, I will give men in exchange for you, and people in exchange for your life. (Isaiah 43:1–4)

We may not be nearly as indispensable as we think we are, but we're more beloved than we ever dreamed of being. God looks for those of us whose hearts are fully committed to Him. And when He finds us, He strengthens us.

Ultimately, godly wisdom is found in two simple truths: It's not all about us, and it's not all up to us. Let's remember God's faithfulness, trust in His strength, and rest in His refuge. Then and only then will we really be wise.

Hopeful Reflections

1. What movies have you been showing at your me-MAX theater? _____

    _____

    _____

    _____

    _____

    _____

2. Do *you* consume your thoughts more than anyone or anything else? _____

    _____

    _____

    _____

    _____

    _____

    _____

3. What "sandwiches" are bearing down on you right now?

    _____

    _____

4. Do you struggle with trying to win the races in your life all by yourself? _____

    _____

    _____

    _____

    _____

    _____

5. Make a mental list of the most pressing concerns in your
    life right now. Read Psalm 31 and pray that God will
    help you trust that He is your rock and your refuge—and
    that every part of your life is safe in His hands. _____

    _____

    _____

    _____

    _____

    _____

    _____

    _____

What then is the chief end of man?
Man's chief end is to glorify God
and to enjoy Him forever.

—The Westminster Larger Catechism, 1861

ELEVEN

The Gift of Worship

Hiking toward Moriah

I've already mentioned that my friend Kim came to Nashville to pursue a career in music. Her dream came true, and she's been a professional musician for more than ten years. She records albums, gives concerts, and has her songs played on the radio. But she also sings when no one is listening. She sings when she vacuums, she sings in the car, she sings on her bike, she sings when she's working on her computer. Her parents will tell you that she started singing when she was a toddler, and she's never stopped. It's almost as if music plays continuously in her mind; singing seems as natural to her as breathing. It's her gift.

I think worship should be like that for Christian women. Worship should be as natural as breathing for us. It's our gift to God. But unfortunately, some of us withhold our gift of worship from Him because we don't really understand what it is. Worship is not only unnatural for some of us; it's a frighteningly foreign concept. So we're going to spend this chapter demystifying worship—talking about what it is, what it isn't, and how we can live a lifestyle of worship.

The Wonder of Worship

The most frequently used Greek verb translated into "worship" in Scripture is *proskuneo*. It's derived from the root words *pros*, which means "toward," and *kuneo*, which means "to kiss."[1] *Proskuneo* reminds me of a guy named Jerry whom I had a huge crush on in college. We took a few long walks around campus together that always ended chastely in front of my dorm. And there, under a big magnolia tree, Jerry would lean toward me and pray sincere, eloquent prayers. Of course I didn't pay attention to the words he was winging heavenward, because I was thinking that he should come toward me a little closer and give me a big kiss!

Unlike the unrequited crush I had on Jerry, the biblical word picture that *proskuneo* paints is one of sweet and reverent adoration of a loving Savior. It's the word Jesus used for worship in His conversation with the Samaritan woman at the well. She knew all about moving toward men and kissing them. Her diary was full of old flames, probably even a "Jerry" or two. But the objects of her affection weren't worthy of worship, and she was left with a parched heart and a dry soul. It wasn't until Jesus quenched her thirst with streams of living water that she understood the true meaning of worship (John 4:21–24).

Another description of worship is found in a proverb that we're most likely to hear our pastors quote in their annual sermon series on tithing:

> Honor the LORD with your wealth, with the firstfruits of all your crops; then your barns will be filled to overflowing, and your vats will brim over with new wine. (Proverbs 3:9–10)

This verse refers to a Jewish ceremony involving the sacrificial offering of "firstfruits." A firstfruit was the most perfect, unblemished fruit, wine, grain, or oil from an Israelite's crop. It was the first and the best he or she had to offer. I've written the words *mind and heart* next to the word *wealth* in the margin of my Bible at Proverbs 3:9. The concept of giving someone (or something) the firstfruits of our attention and affection—the very best of our time and love—has become my favorite definition of worship. And when I lay that definition across the activity of my life, it becomes obvious that I worship lots of things other than God. I give Him some of my attention and affection, but usually not the firstfruits. The firstfruits of my mind and heart are usually sacrificed at the altar of "me."

What about you? Does God get your firstfruits? Or does something or someone else get the best of your time and love?

I WORSHIP LOTS OF THINGS OTHER THAN GOD. I GIVE HIM SOME OF MY ATTENTION AND AFFECTION, BUT USUALLY NOT THE FIRSTFRUITS.

The Moral of Moriah

The Old Testament story of Abraham and Isaac offers a convicting lesson on worship. Abraham was a man of faith; four verses in Hebrews 11 (sometimes referred to as the "Hall of Faith" chapter) are spent recounting his faithfulness. He was obedient to God's direction even when he had no idea where God was leading him. He certainly gave the Lord a lot of attention and affection. But he also gave a great deal of attention and affection to his son Isaac.

Isaac's birth was the fulfillment of a promise God had made to Abraham and Sarah. He was the child they thought they'd never have—not even in their wildest dreams. They actually laughed at the prospect. They just couldn't imagine buying Pampers when they were both wearing Depends! But the Bible says, "God is not a man, that he should lie" (Numbers 23:19), and Isaac was born according to God's plan when Abraham was one hundred years old.

Can you just imagine the new parents' complete amazement and delight when Isaac bellowed his first cry? They probably fought over who got to change his diapers. And I'll bet they never took him to Mother's Day Out! He was their beloved, only son. They couldn't get enough of him. His name literally means "laughter" in Hebrew—and appropriately so, because he was the joy of their lives.

Thus Abraham's heart sank when God asked him to sacrifice this precious boy, his laughter, on the altar of Mount Moriah.

Then God said, "Take your son, your only son, Isaac, whom you love, and go to the region of Moriah. Sacrifice him there as a burnt offering on one of the mountains I will tell you about." (Genesis 22:2)

I'm sure the depth of Abraham's sorrow that day was as great as the joy he had in the delivery tent. But he was obedient. Scripture tells us he got up early the next morning and saddled his donkey. I think he got up early because he wanted to avoid a morning coffee chat with Sarah. How in the world was he going to tell her that he planned to kill their son? Abraham had a long time to think about it while he trudged with Isaac through the desert to the region of Moriah, which was three days away.

On the third day of their journey, Abraham wearily looked up from his sandals and saw Mount Moriah in the distance. He probably wished with all his heart that it was a mirage. I wonder if his face betrayed his anguish when he told the servants to stay behind with the donkeys while he and Isaac went to the mountain to worship:

> Abraham took the wood for the burnt offering and placed it on his son Isaac, and he himself carried the fire and the knife. As the two of them went on together, Isaac spoke up and said to his father, Abraham, "Father?"
> "Yes, my son?" Abraham replied.
> "The fire and the wood are here," Isaac said, "but where is the lamb for the burnt offering?" (Genesis 22:6–7)

I can't begin to imagine the agony that pierced

Abraham's heart when Isaac asked him about the lamb. The boy had seen his dad perform dozens of ceremonial sacrifices; he knew a lamb was the proper sacrifice for a burnt offering. And he also knew they hadn't brought one with them from their pens back home. But he didn't argue when Abraham told him that God Himself would provide the lamb. And it doesn't appear that Isaac struggled when they reached the top of the mountain, where it became obvious that *he* was going to be the offering. His dad was well over one hundred years old—certainly not strong enough to subdue the boy physically. Isaac's sweet submission surely cut Abraham's already broken heart like a knife:

> When they reached the place God had told him about, Abraham built an altar there and arranged wood on it. He bound his son Isaac and laid him on the altar, on top of the wood. Then he reached out his hand and took the knife to slay his son. (Genesis 22:9–10)

Of course you know the rest of the story. God provided the greatest gift Abraham could have imagined in the form of a ram trapped in a thicket. That auspicious animal was the perfect substitute for a burnt offering. Old Abraham probably bawled during the barbecue because he was so thankful that he didn't have to slay his own son. The story has a very happy ending.

But why do you think there is a story in the first place? Why do you think God asked Abraham to go through that horrible journey and contemplate such a heartbreaking sacrifice? I think this story is an Old Testament masterpiece depicting how we are supposed to adore Abba, our heavenly Father. I think God was reminding Abraham—and the rest of us—that He is the only one worthy of our worship. Isaac needed attention and affection from his dad, but he wasn't entitled to the firstfruits of Abraham's time and love.

Several years ago my mother told me about her own Moriah moment. It happened one humid June afternoon when I was fifteen. She'd spent the day driving my cousin Brenda and me to a Christian camp three hours away from home. We had been selected to be part of the camp's staff and had to be at orientation the day after we got out of school for summer vacation. I don't remember Mom acting particularly sad when we said good-bye at camp, but I was distracted. I was so excited about being a lifeguard and water-ski instructor that I couldn't wait to put my bags in the musty cabin and change into a bathing suit! I probably just gave her a quick hug and a peck on the cheek and jumped out of the car without a backward glance.

But Mom said she drove away from camp with a heavy heart. She was thinking about how time had flown and how I wasn't her little girl anymore. She realized my college years were right around the corner, and before she knew it I was going to be "away from home" for the rest of my life. She started working in the yard as soon as she arrived back at the house, trying to mow down her misery. After a while she took a shower to clean up. And as soon as the water started running, she started crying. She slid down the tile wall and sat on the shower floor, sobbing for a long time. She was struggling with the same heart-wrenching hurdle that Abraham and other loving parents have jumped over for thousands of years: letting their children go.

Mom says her bathroom breakdown was a pivotal point in her walk with God. He comforted her while she cried and dried her tears with the towel of His truth. He gently convicted her that I had become her Isaac, that she was holding on to me too tightly, that she was giving me the *firstfruits* of her attention and affection. He reminded her that while I was her precious daughter, I was not worthy of her worship.

> I HAVE TO MAKE PILGRIMAGES TO MORIAH ON A REGULAR BASIS AND PLACE THOSE LONGINGS ON THE ALTAR IN ORDER FOR GOD TO REMAIN IN HIS RIGHTFUL PLACE ON THE THRONE OF MY LIFE.

Do you have an Isaac in your life?

I have two: a husband and a child. I long to be married to a good and godly man, and I long to have a little girl or boy call me "Mommy." Sometimes I want those two things more than anything else in the world, and the desire for them becomes the sole focus of my mind and heart. I have to make pilgrimages to

Moriah on a regular basis and place those longings on the altar in order for God to remain in His rightful place on the throne of my life. Desiring marriage and children isn't sinful, but that desire doesn't deserve the best of my time and affection.

Worship Is Vertical, Not Lateral

People aren't created to be idolized. Remember the time in the Book of Acts when Cornelius tried to worship Peter?

> As Peter entered the house, Cornelius met him and fell at his feet in reverence. But Peter made him get up. "Stand up," he said, "I am only a man myself." (Acts 10:25–26)

Ashley Cleveland Greenberg is another one of my talented musical friends. She's got an incredible alto voice and is a passionate guitar picker. She and Kim and I were having coffee a few months ago when she told us a story about misguided worship. It happened when she and her husband, Kenny, were at the Grammy Awards in Hollywood. Ashley had been nominated for a Grammy in the category of Christian Rock Album of the Year. Keep in mind that Christian music is viewed by many people in the industry as a dinky division, not worthy of the television glitz and glamor surrounding the Grammy ceremony. Nonetheless, Ashley was an official Grammy nominee and therefore had to walk the famous red carpet to enter the theater.

She said she and Kenny were feeling pretty silly when their requisite limousine pulled up to the auditorium entrance, which was surrounded by paparazzi. They stepped out into a sea of flashbulbs and were blinded for a moment by the fawning media frenzy taking place behind the velvet ropes. Then Ashley heard one of the photographers ask another, "Who are they?" His fellow shutterbug replied, "Oh, they're nobody." Within seconds, the photographers turned back to their cigarettes and conversations, not wanting to waste their film on "nobodies."

Ashley laughed when she told us about her awards show snub. She said it was a great reminder that people aren't supposed to be worshiped. In fact, worshiping people is dangerous—first for the ones being worshiped, because they might start believing they're worthy of all the adulation. And second for the ones doing the worshiping, because they will surely be disappointed.

Have you ever been disappointed because someone you idolized let you down?

Worship was never meant to be a lateral experience. It's supposed to be vertical:

WORSHIP WAS NEVER MEANT TO BE A LATERAL EXPERIENCE.

Sing to the LORD, all the earth; proclaim his salvation day after day. Declare his glory among the nations, his marvelous deeds among all peoples. For great is the LORD and most worthy of praise; he is to be feared above all gods. For all the gods of the nations are idols, but the LORD made the heavens. Splendor and majesty are before him; strength and joy in his dwelling place. Ascribe to the LORD, O families of nations, ascribe to the LORD glory and strength, ascribe to the LORD the glory due his name. Bring an offering and come before him; worship the LORD in the splendor of his holiness. (1 Chronicles 16:23–29)

Only God is worthy of our worship!

Hopeful Reflections

1. Spend some time alone writing down the top three or four people (or things or desires) to which you give the most attention and affection._____

_____

_____

_____

_____

_____

_____

2. Pray over each person or thing and ask God to reveal if this represents an "Isaac" in your life. _____

_____

_____

_____

_____

_____

3. Read John 4:23–24. What do you think Jesus meant by saying, "True worshipers will worship the Father in spirit and truth"? Which aspect of worship do you gravitate toward: spirit (emotive) or truth (pragmatic)? _____

_____

_____

_____

_____

_____

4. Consider doing a biblical word study on *worship*, using a topical concordance and a good Bible commentary.

_____

_____

_____

_____

_____

_____

5. If you have $10–$15 you can part with, buy a worship CD or cassette tape and spend some time alone listening to the lyrics and singing praises to the Lord—even if He's the only One who thinks your noise is joyful! (My favorite worship recordings are by Kim Hill, Darlene Zschech/Hillsongs, the Vineyard Winds of Worship series, Matt Redmond, Rita Springer, and the W.O.W. Worship series.)

The indispensable condition for developing
and maintaining the awareness of our belovedness is
time alone with God.

—Brennan Manning

TWELVE

Wooed by His Love

Serenaded by a Savior

About ten years ago a good friend (who shall remain nameless to preserve his reputation) set me up on a blind date with an enthusiastic preacher we'll call Bob. Our first date was lunch at an elegant restaurant. Bob was the perfect suitor until he bowed his head to bless our meal. The discourse that bellowed forth was by far the loudest prayer that I've ever heard in an expensive eating establishment. Bob not only thundered his thanks for the food, he went on to favorably comment on my character as a godly woman—which of course was conjecture on his part, since we'd just met! I didn't feel very godly as I forced myself to remain seated with my eyes closed and resist the temptation to slip away and call a cab as he continued. The rest of our lunch together is a blur.

Following that one and only official date, Bob was relentless in his pursuit of me. He sent flowers, wrote letters, and did all kinds of things to communicate his affection. He even serenaded me with songs on the answering machine!

Although my response to his courting wasn't very positive, he still seemed determined to be the best beau he could be. Shakespeare would've been proud, because Bob pitched some serious woo.

But even Bob's passionate fervor pales next to the Lover of our souls. God plants vivid panoramas of wildflowers for our pleasure. He writes living letters reminding us of His love. And He serenades us with songs of delight and deliverance. We should rejoice with wonder at being wooed by the Lord of the universe!

Avoiding the Bondage of Busyness

I've discovered (with the help of a prophet, masquerading as a Christian counselor named Ken) that I'm not very good at being wooed. I have a hard time enjoying God's gifts, savoring the sweetness of His letters, and listening quietly while His love songs play in my mind. I have a performance-oriented personality that leans toward having way too many irons in the proverbial fire, resulting in chaotic busyness. The constant static and activity of my life make lingering and listening difficult, leaving me a weak "woo-ee." I've only recently begun to practice the disciplines of resting and finding refuge so my heart will be pliant for His pursuit. I want to live as a woman being wooed by God!

I doubt if many of us get enough rest. And by rest, I mean experiencing an interval of unhurried peace that consumes our body, mind, and spirit. In other words, our hands and our hearts are quiet and content—still before God. By that definition, what I call rest is better described as complete collapse. I typically go as hard as I can until I run out of gas, then I break down on the side of the road. Just as soon as I can refill my tank—with whatever it takes to get started again—I'm back out on the road, going just as fast as I did before the breakdown. Mechanics will tell you that kind of stress destroys engines in a short amount of time. If the only rest you're getting is the inactivity resulting from a breakdown, your spiritual life is going to burn out before you know it.

IF THE ONLY REST YOU'RE GETTING IS THE INACTIVITY RESULTING FROM A BREAKDOWN, YOUR SPIRITUAL LIFE IS GOING TO BURN OUT BEFORE YOU KNOW IT.

Two years ago I had a wonderful job with Focus on the Family. Focus is a fantastic organization, and I was honored to be on staff, doing what I loved. I got to travel all over the country directing and speaking at women's retreats, encouraging women in their walk with the Lord. Working there was a great experience that left my heart full of precious memories. However, because of my tendency to choose busyness over rest, I began to neglect private time with God in order to work harder in public. I ignored the cry of my soul for spiritual restoration and rejuvenation and worked relentlessly at ministry. I sinned by saturating myself with more and more responsibilities.

Yet God was patient with my prideful pace. He effectively

wooed and impressed me that I needed to give up working for Him in order to spend more time with Him. I'm slowly learning that true spiritual rest—*being alone with God*—is more important than my productivity.

A good friend of mine stays extremely busy in her work for another wonderful ministry. She, too, flies all over the country telling people about Jesus. Conversations with her are often interrupted by a shrill cell phone demanding her immediate attention. She is completely sold-out to the Lord—and she is completely exhausted. The last time we were together, she was drinking enough caffeine to choke a horse in order to keep up the frenetic pace. For a moment I was tempted to join her; I knew I'd lose about ten pounds in a week with her schedule! But I'm not willing to sacrifice the peace I've discovered in God's sanctuary of rest. I'm afraid the noise of such a life would drown out the songs He sings to woo me.

I'M SLOWLY LEARNING THAT TRUE SPIRITUAL REST—BEING ALONE WITH GOD—IS MORE IMPORTANT THAN MY PRODUCTIVITY.

Does the busyness of your life muffle God's love song to you?

As His beloved but busy daughters, we must learn that our souls require rest. In order to be wooed by God, we have to be willing to surrender our busyness for a season. A seventeenth-century French archbishop named Fénelon wrote about our need to be still with incredible insight, long before drive-through windows and cell phones added to an already chaotic culture:

> When it comes to accomplishing things for God, you will find that high aspirations, enthusiastic feelings, careful planning, and being able to express yourself well are not worth very much. The important thing is absolute surrender to God. You can do anything He wants you to do if you are walking in the light of full surrender.[1]

IN ORDER TO BE WOOED BY GOD, WE HAVE TO BE WILLING TO SURRENDER OUR BUSYNESS FOR A SEASON.

I think the scary thing about surrendering to rest is that it involves another s-word: *submission*. It involves yielding to the reality that we're not invincible or indispensable. Facing the fact that we're tired, and we really can't make it by ourselves. Recognizing that we need some spiritual nourishment and a nap. Admitting that we've pulled on our bootstraps until they've broken, and now we can't make it up the hill in front of us. Submission means abdicating total control of our lives and living in the harsh reality that we aren't the rulers of our universe.

Surrendering to His Sovereignty

David's reputation heralds him as the greatest king who ever lived, but many would argue that his greatness was forged in the crucible of submission. One of the best books I've read on the subject of submission and resting in God's sovereignty follows the story of David from boy to aging monarch. Chapter 11 of *A Tale of Three Kings* by Gene Edwards gives us some powerful pointers regarding rest:

> Caves are not the ideal place for morale building. There is a certain sameness to them all, no matter how many you have lived in. Dark. Wet. Cold. Stale. A cave becomes even worse when you are its sole inhabitant...and in the distance you can hear dogs baying.
>
> But sometimes, when the dogs and hunters were not near, the prey sang. He [David, hunted by Saul] started low, then lifted up his voice and sang the song the little lamb had taught him. The cavern walls echoed each note just as the mountains once had done. The music rolled down into deep cavern darkness that soon became an echoing choir singing back to him.
>
> He had less now than he had when he was a shepherd, for now he had no lyre, no sun, not even the company of sheep. The memories of the court had faded. David's greatest ambition now reached no higher than a shepherd's staff. Everything was being crushed out of him.
>
> He sang a great deal.
>
> And matched each note with a tear.
>
> How strange, is it not, what suffering begets?
>
> There in those caves, drowned in the sorrow of his song, and in the song of his sorrow, David very simply became the greatest hymn writer and the greatest comforter of broken hearts this world shall ever know.[2]

I believe David was a great king because he understood that his throne was just a chair in God's sovereign floor plan. He didn't boast that he was invincible, and he didn't seem to worry about being indispensable. He knew the business of ruling Israel would be just fine without him. He was a submissive servant who worked hard for God's glory but also ran to Him for rest. He learned to leave the palace policies on his desk, turn off his cell phone, and lie down in green pastures. He never wanted for wooing.

How about you? Do you spend enough time resting in the presence of God to recognize His voice?

Seeking Sanctuary

How do we find a refuge in the midst of our busy lives where we can rest and be still before God? The story of Elijah's wilderness survival vacation gives us a clue. Immediately following his prophecy to King Ahab, Elijah the Tishbite (sounds like "fishbite"!) was told by God to hide in a ravine near the Jordan River. He did as he was told and hiked to the Kerith Kampgrounds:

> Now Elijah the Tishbite, from Tishbe in Gilead, said to Ahab, "As the LORD, the God of Israel, lives, whom I serve, there will be neither dew nor rain in the next few years except at my word."
> Then the word of the LORD came to Elijah: "Leave here, turn eastward and hide in the Kerith Ravine, east of the Jordan. You will drink from the brook, and I have ordered ravens to feed you there."
> So he did what the LORD had told him. He went to the Kerith Ravine, east of the Jordan, and stayed there. The ravens brought him bread and meat in the morning and bread and meat in the evening, and he drank from the brook. (1 Kings 17:1–6)

Chapter 12: *Wooed by His Love*　　179

While all of Israel was suffering from a famine brought on by their obsession with Baal, God sustained Elijah. He satisfied his hunger with food delivered by a friendly flock of ravens. (Let's not pause to think about what kind of "food" it was!) And He quenched the obedient prophet's thirst with sweet water from a babbling brook. God miraculously protected and provided for His servant. He gave Elijah refuge in a ravine.

God has given me refuge in a rope and canvas hammock chair. I bought this cute, green-and-white-striped swing from Brookstone after wanting it for a year. I justified the purchase by deciding it would be the perfect place to practice the discipline of resting! I hung it from a big, red-leaf maple tree in my backyard. It's not much of an exaggeration to say that chair has changed my life. Better yet, it has changed my heart.

I try to spend at least a few minutes each night sitting in the chair. In fact, most evenings find me out in the backyard swinging before I get ready for bed. I try to be completely quiet in my heart and mind and just listen for His voice. Sometimes I can see the moon and stars filtering through the branches above me. This summer I've watched ardent male fireflies flash yellow and green in a dazzling dance for a maiden's favor. I can usually hear the conversation of crickets and sometimes the rumble of a train in the distance. And I've learned to hear God.

HE DOESN'T SPEAK TO ME AUDIBLY, BUT HIS VOICE IS UNMISTAKABLE.

He doesn't speak to me audibly, but His voice is unmistakable. My silent perch has become a place of merciful provision. He nourishes me with His nearness and comforts me with His Spirit while I sway back and forth.

Several weeks ago I was with some women who've had box-seat views of my life for the last two years. I teach a weekly Bible study at their company and typically use lots of personal anecdotes to illustrate scriptural points. That makes them privy to my good days and bad days, whether they like it or not! Anyway, we were talking about what spiritual contentment looks like, and one of the women—a jewel named Mandy—said, "Lisa, you seem different now. You're so much more peaceful and rested." I was really glad it showed. As the wise man said:

> As water reflects a face, so a man's heart reflects the man. (Proverbs 27:19)

All the time spent watching glimmering fireflies and thanking the One who made them had given me a soft glow too. We are changed when we spend time alone in His presence!

Where is your special place of refuge? Do you have somewhere to go to be alone with God?

Maybe you need to buy a swinging hammock chair or put candles in a quiet corner of a special room or find some other way to create a place of sanctuary. Swaying is optional! My prayer for you echoes the words of Paul:

Chapter 12: *Wooed by His Love*   181

And this is my prayer: that your love may abound more and more in knowledge and depth of insight, so that you may be able to discern what is best and may be pure and blameless until the day of Christ, filled with the fruit of righteousness that comes through Jesus Christ—to the glory and praise of God. (Philippians 1:9–11)

We all need to take the time and find a place to be alone with our heavenly Father. It is only in our rest and in His refuge that we become women wooed by our Redeemer. He tenders our hearts when we take time to marinate in His mercy. And that cherished communion with Him indelibly imprints us as His daughters—desperate for mercy, defined by grace, and beloved by God.

Hopeful Reflections

1. Read Psalm 23 out loud by yourself. Have you spent enough time resting by still waters to hear God's voice?

_____

_____

_____

_____

_____

_____

2. Meditate on Psalm 32:7; Zephaniah 3:17; and Isaiah 62:5. It might help to write these verses on index cards or Post-It notes and put them somewhere noticeable.

_____

_____

_____

_____

_____

3. Find, build, buy, or create a special "sanctuary" where you can be still and marinate in His mercy._____

_____

_____

_____

_____

4. Share your desire to be a better "woo-ee" with a close Christian friend or mentor. Ask that person to help keep you accountable for spending regular time in your sanctuary alone with God. _____

_____

_____

_____

_____

_____

_____

5. Read *The Sacred Romance* by John Eldredge (Thomas Nelson/Word Publishers). It's an incredible book about intimacy with God. (Hint: It's best when savored slowly!)_____

_____

_____

_____

_____

_____

_____

_____

Notes

Chapter One

1. C. S. Lewis, *Letters to Malcolm: Chiefly on Prayer* (New York: Harcourt Brace Jovanovich, 1964), 69.

Chapter Three

1. Philip Yancey, *What's So Amazing about Grace?* (Grand Rapids, Mich.: Zondervan, 1997), 49–51.

Chapter Four

1. Yohanan Aharoni and Michael Avi-Yonah, *The Macmillan Bible Atlas* (New York: Macmillan, 1968), 146.

Chapter Seven

1. Victor Harold Matthews, *Manners and Customs in the Bible* (Peabody, Mass.: Hendrickson, 1988), 259–60.

Chapter Eight

1. Craig L. Blomberg, *Interpreting the Parables* (Downer's Grove, Ill.: InterVarsity Press, 1990), 193–96.

2. Alan D. Wright, *Lover of My Soul* (Sisters, Ore.: Multnomah, 1998), 81–83.

Chapter Nine

1. Craig L. Blomberg, *Jesus and the Gospels* (Nashville, Tenn.: Broadman & Holman, 1997), 165–72.

Chapter Ten

1. A. W. Tozer, *The Pursuit of God* (Harrisburg, Penn.: Christian Publications, 1948).

Chapter Eleven

1. W. E. Vine, Merrill F. Unger, and William White, Jr., *Vine's Complete Expository Dictionary of Old and New Testament Words* (Nashville, Tenn.: Thomas Nelson, 1984, 1996), 686.

Chapter Twelve

1. Fénelon, *Let Go* (New Kensington, Penn.: Whitaker, 1973), 35.

2. Gene Edwards, *A Tale of Three Kings* (Auburn, Maine: Christian Books, 1980), 27–28.